THE AUTHOR

Kenneth Hudson is the author of more than twenty books on social and industrial topics. He was a university lecturer at Bristol and Bath for twelve years, and for a further twelve a producer and industrial correspondent with the BBC. The present book is based on many years' close acquaintance with people who are involved, at a responsible level, with a country's ability to earn a living and to govern itself.

Kenneth Hudson has travelled and lectured a great deal, both in Europe and North America, and is consequently in an unusually favourable position to make useful comparisons of the calibre and public performance of senior executives on both sides of the Atlantic. His present work as a UNESCO consultant has allowed him to enlarge this experience to Africa, South America and the Far East.

The Businessman in Public

The Businessman in Public

KENNETH HUDSON

A HALSTED PRESS BOOK

JOHN WILEY & SONS
New York – Toronto

English language edition, except USA and Canada
published by
Associated Business Programmes Ltd
17 Buckingham Gate, London SWI

Published in USA and Canada by
Halsted Press, a Division of
John Wiley & Sons Inc
New York

First published 1976

Library of Congress Cataloging in Publication Data

Hudson, Kenneth.
    The businessman in public.

        "A Halsted Press book."
        Includes index.
        1.   Executives – Great Britain.   2.   Public relations –
Great Britain.   I.   Title.
HF5500.3.G7H83   1975   658.4'00941   75-40414

ISBN 0-470-01377-X

Printed in Great Britain by Lowe & Brydone (Printers) Ltd
Thetford, Norfolk

Contents

INTRODUCTION

Meaning of 'the businessman' and 'in public'

'Businessman' is not a name which everyone employed in business matters finds flattering. It is, on the whole, easier to use in America than in Britain without giving offence, but in both countries it acquires a steadily more right-wing flavour each year. Here we have decided to use it merely as a convenient label, for which we can find no effective substitute. For the purposes of this book a businessman is taken to be someone working at a senior executive level within the broad fields of industry, commerce, finance, the professions and the public services; the person with the money to take two vacations a year instead of one, even if he chooses not to; the fortunate individual whose services are likely to be retained during a recession. At the British summit level, this is the kind of person referred to by *The Times* under its headline, 'Peerage and nine knighthoods for businessmen in honours list'* – the managing director of Fairey Engineering; the president of the CBI; the deputy governor of the Bank of England; the managing director of Vickers; the chairman and managing director of the George Cohen 600 group; a partner in Husband and Company, consulting engineers; the chairman of Booker McConnell; the chairman of the British Airways Board.

The complete law mix would also include the higher ranks of the police, the law, the Civil Service and local government. We are thinking, in general terms, of the people who run the

---

*June 14, 1975

nation's affairs, receive the top salaries and are, to a certain extent, interchangeable, although a good deal less so in Britain than in some other countries. Even in Britain, however, it is fairly normal for men to move from the Civil Service and the professions to the boards of banks, insurance and finance companies, and manufacturing industries. In the United States, it is even more normal and in France the products of the principal institutions of higher education, the Grandes Écoles, expect to control everything and on the whole do, with much sideways movement between the public and private sectors.

'Businessman' is, in fact, a convenient shorthand term for the 50,000 or so men, and perhaps 1,000 women, who occupy the most responsible positions in any European country. They are the people who direct a country's business, and the nature of the political system has remarkably little to do with either their existence or their power, influence and prestige. In our sense of the term, 'businessmen' in Poland or Hungary have much the same problems and opportunities, both private and public, as 'businessmen' in the United States or Britain.

'In public' can be simply defined as 'in situations when one is not talking only to one's immediate colleagues or professional associates'. Such occasions may range from after-dinner speeches to television interviews, and from brains trusts to opening village fêtes. They are the times when one is not protected by rank, tradition or house-conventions or by any form of protective clothing, the times when one is on one's own, revealed in all the naked loneliness of a good or bad performer.

1. The social and educational background of British businessmen

From an international point of view, there is no such thing as a 'normal' or 'average' businessman, although a hundred men and women carrying considerable executive responsibility in Bulgaria would probably turn out to have a not dissimilar bundle of personal qualities from a hundred similarly placed people in Canada or the Netherlands. For practical reasons, one has to use this or that country as a yardstick and since the present author is British and this book is being published in Britain, it seems not unreasonable to use the British business-man as one's main laboratory specimen. Readers in other countries will find it, one hopes, a worthwhile and stimulating task to note the ways in which their own national specimens differ from the British. Where, an American or a German may feel inclined to ask, were a sample fifty of his own industrial executives educated? What did their fathers do? What do they look and sound like? What sort of things do they do when they are not working? There is no shortage of reference books to supply him with the answers, once his curiosity is aroused.

Even now, in 1975, and after all the opportunities for higher education which have existed for the past fifty years, British businessmen in the productive and moneymaking concerns are a curiously-assorted group. The self-made man who left school at 14 is still commonly found at the top of large indus-trial and commercial undertakings in Britain, although he has become a comparative rarity elsewhere in Europe and even, despite the carefully preserved folklore of American business, in the United States. He is almost unknown in Japan and he is being rapidly phased out in the countries of the Eastern bloc, as the growing supply of technically trained managers makes the chief-executive-from-the-ranks type obsolete and unnecessary.

Mr John Gregson, who received a Life Peerage in 1975, is an interesting bridge-figure between the old and the new worlds of industry. He joined the Fairey Group as an office-boy when he was 15. Soon afterwards he began an apprenticeship with the company as a draughtsman and in 1946, when he was 22, he joined Fairey's research and development team which was working on the then new technology of nuclear power. Obviously a man of exceptional ability, he was given overall responsibility for the company's work on the Trawsfynydd Nuclear Power Station and in 1966 he was appointed to the board of the Group's nuclear engineering subsidiary, in charge of general engineering activities. He became managing director in October 1974, and, in addition to his position with the Fairey Group, he is vice-chairman of the Production Engineering Research Association.

If he had been born twenty years later, he would almost certainly have found his way to a university with great ease, probably to take a degree in engineering. The generation of managers pushing up behind him is for the most part made up of graduate engineers. Lord Gregson belongs to a powerful, but dying breed. It would be impertinent and quite wrong to suggest that he is uneducated – one can acquire one's education in a variety of ways – but it would certainly be fair to say that he, like hundreds of other talented men and women in his age group, did not receive all the formal education he deserved. One of the more interesting results of this is that he sounds classless, which, in the political and social melting-pot of modern Britain, can be one of a man's greatest advantages.

It is illuminating to compare Lord Gregson's career and background with those of British industrialists as a whole. It is not easy to round up British businessmen and to study them as a group, but certain attempts have been made. Every three years since 1967 the British Institute of Management has carried out an investigation into the composition of the boards of a hundred leading companies. There appears to have been a remarkably small amount of change over the period. In 1967 71 per cent of the directors had been educated at a public school. The figures for 1970 and 1973 were precisely the same, from which one is bound to conclude that the chances of a former State school pupil being elected a director of a prestigious company are showing little signs of improving. The tone, manner, tastes, creed and speech of the boards of these and many other companies is that of the English public school. Other significant details revealed in these reports are:

	1967 (%)	*1970* (%)	*1973* (%)
Professionally qualified	27	32	35
Family connexions with company	17	15	17
Educated at Oxford or Cambridge	32	32	29
Educated at other universities	19	20	20
Attended a business school	18	9	8

A rather earlier survey, commissioned by the Institute of Directors[1] and published in 1965 was based on a much larger sample – 10,000 of its members – but showed a similar picture. There were, however, important differences between the generations. Of those directors born between 1890 and 1899, 32.9 per cent had been to a public school and 18 per cent to a university, but for the age-group 1930–39 the figures were 75.4 per cent for a public school and 27.4 per cent for a university.

The Institute was able to discover a good deal of information about professional qualifications. Broadly speaking, the bigger the company, the higher was the proportion of qualified people. Much the highest, among directors, was for chartered accountants. These, in Britain, are reckoned to be particularly worthy of promotion to high office in business, but on the Continent and in America the technical man is considered more desirable.

An analysis of fifty leaders of industry, commerce and finance whose personal details are given in the 1975 edition of

Who's Who allows us to round out and correct the picture a little, and to put some colour into it. 64 per cent of these successful and influential figures had been knighted, 12 per cent had peerages, 42 per cent had been to a public school, 28 per cent to either Oxford or Cambridge and 14 per cent to another university. *Who's Who*, one realises, is concerned only with the most eminent people and, for this reason, any details gathered from its pages are not strictly comparable with those gleaned by the British Institute of Management or the Institute of Directors, whose raw material necessarily includes both the dull and the run-of-the-mill, as well as the highly successful. The *Who's Who* group, in any case, contains a number – Lord Bernstein, Nigel Broakes, Sir Raymond Brookes, Raymond Burton, Sir Charles Clore, Sydney Ellis, Maxwell Joseph, Sir Joseph Lockwood, Sir Don Ryder, Sir Jules Thorn – who gave no information as to their education and a smaller number – Sir John Cohen, Sir Lew Grade, and Sir Isaac Wolfson – who registered the fact, possibly with some pride, that their schooling had ended at a very early age.

It is doubtful, however, if the 1985 edition of *Who's Who* will show the same proportion of business leaders who left school at the earliest possible moment. Lord Bernstein, Sir John Cohen and their contemporaries may belong to the last generation of vigorous and strongly entrepreneurial types who rose to riches and influence by their own efforts, unsupported by educational qualifications. Nevertheless, the difference between the educational background of the *Who's Who* group and the samples studied by the Institute of Directors and the British Institute of Management is interesting and, from some points of view, depressing, since there is evidently a strong chance that our most successful businessmen will have had only the legal minimum of formal education. As we shall see in a later chapter, this is what many members of the general public believe anyway. In Britain, money-making and a high level of education do not, in the popular mind, frequently occur together.

Men who are successful in business in Britain may be envied

and possibly even respected for their money, their energy and their enterprise, but, understandably, their social prestige is not high. As Michael Fores and David Clark have pointed out recently,[2] the forceful, ruthless and uneducated fill a vacuum in British industry. In the United States and continental Europe a much larger proportion of graduates from the highest-ranking educational institutions go into business, compared with Britain. British managers are, in general, less well educated and less likely to have had a technical training than their counterparts in the other industrially advanced countries. Not surprisingly, therefore, as attempts to rate various occupations and professions by their prestige in the eyes of schoolboys show, engineering and management have a lower prestige in Britain than elsewhere. Their personal characteristics and their style of life are not regarded as particularly admirable.

Whether or not Sir Charles Clore and Sir Jules Thorn represent the last of a long line of self-made tycoons, only the next ten years will tell. What seems certain, however, is that the chief executives of major British companies are, at the moment, distinctly on the elderly side and that some very impatient and frustrated younger men must be waiting eagerly for their death or retirement. One hundred of them, taken consecutively from an up-to-date edition of a standard work of reference, are distributed among the age-groups as follows:

Date of birth	*Percentage of total*
1900 or earlier	1
1901–1910	33
1911–1920	29
1921–1930	28
1931–1940	7
1941–1950	2

This means that, in 1975, only 9 per cent of the chief executives of British industry were below 45 years of age and only 37 per cent below 55. 35.8 per cent, an alarmingly high figure,

of the 45 and over group appear to have had no form of full-
time higher education. For better or for worse, they had learnt
on the job. 'Learning on the job' can, of course, include gaining professional qualifications on the job and an unknown
proportion of these 100 managing directors, possibly as high
as the British Institute of Management's 27–35 per cent, will
have become chartered accountants, cost accountants and
barristers in their spare time, while earning a living. Some, too,
will undoubtedly have acquired a Higher National Diploma
in engineering in the same part-time way.

It may be true, as a Unilever report[3] suggested in the early
1960s, that 'the quality of the manager of the future will
depend much more on sheer brain power and integrity than
it has done in the past, since knowledge will be relatively more
important than the ability to be a nice fella.' For the survival
of the country's economy, one would hope to see such a
change occur sooner rather than later, but at the present time
British management appears to be holding on to its traditional
habits and privileges with some tenacity. Class divisions in
industry and commerce are still very marked. Here, as in other
fields of the national life, one can easily be deceived by changes
in social fashions, especially in accent and dress, which may
appear to be evidence of a more democratic spirit, but which
are, in fact, superficial and of no great significance. In the field
of recruitment to the highest posts, and especially to the Board,
industry remains, in Simon Caulkin's excellent phrase, 'both
the clearest reflexion and the strongest reinforcement of class
attitudes in this country, with the possible exception of the
educational system'.[4]

This is not just a matter of expensive cars, large houses and
food and drink paid for by the company. To obtain a proper
understanding of the mystique and the privileges of the traditional director's world, or perhaps one should say the director's
fantasy world, a skim through the files of *The Director* can be
recommended. The advertisements are particularly helpful.

'Harrods', said an announcement in 1969,[5] 'are proud to
announce the opening of the new Desmond Groves Portrait

Studio. Desmond Groves specialises in Executive Portraiture and our studio has been designed by him exclusively for the Director and the Executive.

'Here you can be photographed in a restful atmosphere with backgrounds and furnishings specially designed for executive portraiture and particularly with Board Room portraiture in mind.'

One can only speculate on what Executive and Board Room Portraiture might be and on the ways in which it might differ from any other kind of portraiture. Is the style different? Does the photographer possess some special skill and understanding which encourages his subject to cultivate a particular kind of expression on his face, a subtle blend of firmness, ruthlessness, knowing one's own mind and warm concern for the welfare of one's subordinates which will make the public and his colleagues realise that the man whose portrait faces them is every inch an executive, a man born and trained to command? Is Mr Groves, in that case, equally good with bishops, generals and chief constables who are, after all, executives in their own fashion? Or is his technique and the décor of his studio designed only for men who have risen fast and high in the world of business? Are there, one wonders, other specialists who concentrate their attentions on religious executives, law and order executives, military executives and town-hall executives, and who have just the right studio background and patter to put these people at their ease and to bring out all that is best in them, with never a touch of the trendy in the atmosphere? Or dare one be so irreverent, cynical and iconoclastic as to suppose that Executive Portraiture is no more than portraits of people who happen to be executives? In that case, the photographer's skill will certainly include the ability to make unprepossessing people look rather more presentable. It cannot surely be an accident that such a high proportion of rich, self-made men on both sides of the Atlantic are so physically ugly. Making a fortune in one generation has always, whether the century is the sixteenth or the twentieth, involved a good deal of harsh, unscrupulous and, at times, semi-legal activity, and a life of this kind undoubtedly leaves its mark on the face. The ugly person has a strong incentive to compensate in some way for the ugliness which would otherwise be an intolerable burden. Ugly women tend to find consolation in good works and in what are nowadays known as the helping careers; ugly men, who cannot all become boxers or comic actors, are very prone to settle for power.

In the British business world, this presents some most interesting, but seldom discussed problems. The law, accountancy and what is called 'the City' – stockbroking, banking, insurance and other traditionally gentlemanly pursuits – are staffed on the executive level almost entirely by people who have not come the whole way in one generation. Most of them belong to families who have always been at least comfortably off and who have taken middle-class values for granted. The property world, on the other hand, and some forms of wholesaling and retailing, contain some very rough diamonds indeed, men who not only are rough diamonds but who take an obvious pride in looking and sounding that way. After observing, both socially and professionally, many hundreds of businessmen, for a number of years, one becomes aware of two distinct breeds and one notices, without any great skill being required, that one is better-looking than the other. The City and the professional type, in general, is a good deal easier on the eye than the self-made tycoon type and, not surprisingly, it is the first, not the second, which usually serves to illustrate the businessman in advertisements.

The children of self-made men are frequently much more agreeable to look at than their fathers. This is, no doubt, partly because they have had a different kind of upbringing – less pinched, less thrusting, less brutal – and, in many cases, partly because the father's money has proved attractive to pretty or handsome potential wives.

The matter of physical appearance will be discussed in much greater detail later. Here it seems necessary to make only two further points, both extremely important. The first is that in Britain certainly, but less obviously in America, there is certainly something which one can not unreasonably call the management face. It has a range of expression and a set of features which comes to a considerable degree from many years of giving orders and holding responsibility. It is different from the great majority of shop-floor faces and the difference can create real psychological problems during both-sides-of-industry discussions, when one breed is facing another across a table, and during television programmes, when the two types of man appear more or less side by side and a comparison is unavoidable. The further back this tradition of responsibility goes in a family, the more certain it is that the current representative will have a management head and a management manner. The armed services expressed the difference as being one of officers and men. It is equally true, and nowadays equally élitist and unpopular, to say that it exists in business, especially in those kinds of industry, like mining, steel-making and car-assembly, where the manual work is hard and exhausting.

From this it will be seen that the apparently small issue of 'executive portraiture' raises a number of fundamental issues. The new generation is exceedingly anxious to look like the people who have been more or less born to the job and, in some instances, this asks a great deal of the photographer, as company public relations departments know to their cost. Accents can, up to a point, be modified, and new habits learned, but one is, to put the point bluntly, stuck with one's face and all it reveals.

The man who is ambitious and who wished to acquire the appropriate protective colouring will take pains to wear the right clothes and glasses, have his hair cut in an approved Institute of Directors style and eat the correct food in the correct places. On these points, too, the advertisements in *The Director* are very helpful. One notices, for example, an advertisement[6] for the Galleon Club (established 1932), which was conveniently close to the Institute of Directors' headquarters in Belgravia. It was 'for gentlemen only, with a membership drawn from directors and executives of industry and the professions', and prospective patrons were assured that 'the Club is synonymous with fine food, wines and perfect service in an atmosphere of luxury and exclusiveness'.

Nobody would suggest that such 'luxury and exclusiveness' has ever formed part of the everyday life of British businessmen, even in the now unbelievably golden days of the 1960s. But, although few would probably care to admit it, fantasy symbols of the Galleon-club type have been a not unimportant element of the daydreams and yearnings of a great many businessmen, the compensations for strikes, militant shop-stewards, falls in the stock market, sales resistance, late deliveries and all the other unpleasant realities of an executive's daily round.

It would be misleading to suggest that only British businessmen need the dream-world of Galleon Restaurants, yachts, expensive medical checks and houses in the sun and fur-covered wives to sustain them and keep them from suicide. *Business Week* and *The New Yorker* provide close parallels to the morale-building of *The Director*. It would seem, even so, that in Britain at least, some forms of morale-building are kept well within reasonable limits. The gin-swigging executive, drowning his sorrows at his employer's expense, appears to have no foundation in fact, unless things have greatly deteriorated since 1970, when the Institute of Directors reported that, of the 8,000 directors and senior executives checked over each year by their Medical Centre, fewer than ten were 'found to be or referred as, alcoholics needing treatment'.[7]

Whether the same would be true of, say, American, German or French businessmen it is difficult to know. If, as seems possible, alcoholism is more likely to hit some occupations than others and to be primarily a disease of the unsuccessful, one might possibly expect senior business executives, who are presumably not short of success, to be able to control their drinking arm rather better than the average. The temptations and opportunities, on the other hand, are – or perhaps one should say in these days of economic depression, have been –

unusually favourable, especially in Britain, where a high proportion of managing directors and similarly high-placed men have hospitality cupboards in their offices and where the pre-lunch bar in the managerial dining-room is normal. Not, one hastens to add, in American offices, where other kinds of arrangements are necessary, usually off the premises. In recent years, however, fear of heart attacks decimating the upper ranks of their staff has caused many firms to launch a strong and sustained campaign against heavy mid-day eating and drinking in high places. The memorable daily occasions in the Guinness Directors' Dining Room at St James's Gate, Dublin, and in many similar places elsewhere are no more. Some large concerns – Marks and Spencer are a good example – have never gone in for these mid-day peaks, with or without guests, at all and so to fall in with the new fashion causes their executives no problems, or no greater problems than previously.

The sad fact remains, even so, that business executives are not, on the whole, a long-lived lot. Some, like employees of the broadcasting companies, die remarkably young. Theories about the causes of early death are, like most other theories, subject to swings of fashion. At one time, the root trouble was supposed to have been heavy eating and lack of exercise, yet heavyweight industrial chairmen such as Lord Netherthorpe and Lord Beeching have outlived the majority of their slim and abstemious colleagues with remarkable success. (The fat vice-president or president is a comparative rarity in the United States.) Frustration and tension are supposed to kill off others and the reality of retirement even more. Musicians, one notes with interest, virtually never retire and, even in today's world, they are an outstandingly long-lived breed, with a God-given extra ration of energy and enthusiasm to carry them through to the end, a bonus which Ford, Carnegie and other great entrepreneurs of capitalism's golden days certainly had, too, but which escapes their successors in the business world, limited and checked by restrictions the pre-1914 world knew little or nothing about.

The advertisers, one supposes, know all this. They have

access to the latest in psychological and sociological research, they know who has the money, they understand current snobberies and aspirations, they monitor the behaviour, the subconscious and the unconscious of their fellow citizens in every possible way, and they presumably apply all this knowledge to the creation of advertising campaigns which will draw the money out of the pockets of the people with most to spare. What then do today's advertisements tell us about the pattern of thinking and feeling and the life style of what we might call, without much distortion or exaggeration, the executive world? What kind of people do the advertisements show as inhabiting that world? What are the pipe-dreams the salesmen hope to turn into cash?

Each country's press reflects its executive class in its own slightly different way. The businessman reflected in *Die Welt* is not quite the same as the businessman of *Le Monde* and both in turn are different from the businessman of *The Times* and *Playboy*. The American businessman shades off into European and the Oriental businessman, but has an identity, shape and flavour of his own, a special set of taboos, facial expressions and priorities. In so far as there is an international mirror for the satisfactions, pleasures, desires and hopes of businessmen, *The New Yorker* is probably closest to it.

What then does *The New Yorker* tell us about today's businessman?[8] Its advertisers, one should state firmly and at the outset, are extremely careful not to give the slightest clue as to the occupations of the people in the pictures. They may be doctors, stockbrokers, publishers, generals, cattle-raisers or lawyers. But they clearly belong to that fortunate upper layer of the population which has few financial worries, which can take a holiday pretty well when and where it wants to, and which is accustomed and anxious to have the best of everything. The advertiser's problem then resolves itself to achieving a definition of 'best' which is satisfactory to all parties, who will necessarily include not only the bronzed, urbanely smiling and well-preserved fifty-year-olds accompanying the text, but their unnaturally beautiful and well-maintained women-folk as well.

These are no first-generation, coarse-grained money-grubbers and so they are naturally in the market for the *Handbook of Gilbert and Sullivan* and for value for money culture-without-too-great-an-effort implied by its blurb ('Never before has a single book contained so much information on the operettas of Gilbert and Sullivan. Best of all, it contains detailed, complete plots of all the operettas.') Their status demands that they should never be caught out over the meaning of a word and, even more important, that they should be able to use them without risk of error or of bringing a smile to the other man's face. So they are naturals for the new Merriam-Webster, America's best-selling dictionary. This, they are relieved and encouraged to hear, 'doesn't just define words. It brings words alive.' So anyone can feel the bitter emptiness of 'rip-off'. And get the full impact of 'chopper'. And at last understand the cool wisdom of 'cryogenics'. With the help of 'over 3000 quotations from poets, comics, critics and presidents', and '24,000 phrases showing you how a word is used in context', no-one need slip up. 'Over 150,000 words spring vividly to life, including 22,000 new ones like "bummer" and "dashiki", as well as the grand old Melvillian polysyllables.'

These are people who prize efficiency. The car to appeal to them is 'redesigned and engineered for the realities of 1975. Its new computerized electronic fuel injection is more efficient than a carburettor. It gives you instant acceleration, great gas mileage and better emission control.' With its 'heritage of superior technology' it is what everyone must surely want, 'the world's most affordable legend'.

Their hi-fi equipment, an important status symbol, has 'a new standard of musical accuracy and an unprecedented degree of placement flexibility', their 92 dollar ball-point pen is 'weighted for proper balance for easy, tireless writing' and its giant cartridge, 'almost $\frac{1}{4}$ in diameter, writes many times longer than conventional cartridges', their home-safe ('secur-

ity vault'), 'engineered for maximum security', is 'virtually
impossible to pry loose from anchor bolts (included)'.

They buy one another 36 inch strings of platinum pearls,
at 18,000 dollars a string, Dior silk ties ('a bit more than a
touch of class'), with a status signature on the bottom, and
75 dollar disc-crests, with the badge of his prestigious car,
'mounted atop the handsome, hand-rubbed teakwood pedes-
tal'. They stock up their homes with Royal Copenhagen
porcelain ('Each piece is signed twice, once by the painter
and once by the gold decorator'), Japanese wood-block prints
and reproductions of the original sand-shakers used by George
Washington at Mount Vernon. If they have really arrived,
they respond to the sentence which tells them, simply and
appealingly, 'what your home could have in common with the
Met, the Tate and the Louvre'. With their interest understandably aroused, they learn that 'beautiful, original works
by artists who are represented in the world's great museums
and galleries can be yours for very reasonable prices. We
offer original etchings, lithographs and serigraphs signed by
Dali, Calder, Clavé, Soyer, Moti, Picasso and other important
artists.'

They go for expensive foreign holidays to places like Dublin, 'a splendidly understated city, infused with country
friendliness', where in a 'vibrant, earthy pub' one can 'get to
grips with a velvet pint of stout for 55 cents', to Switzerland,
where 'the Alps are more than mountains', and to France,
where you can 'eat like a gourmet for pennies, take off for a
lavender field, sit under a cypress, and see a Gothic cathedral
that was a friend's Ph.D. thesis'. Or you can settle for something a little more conventional like the Bahama Out Islands,
where your fellow holidaymakers will be people like yourself,
'Self-reliant. Active. Interesting. And easy to know,' where
your days can be filled with golf and tennis and picking up
shells, and where 'evening brings a casual elegance'.

To describe the icing and decoration on the executive cake
is almost inevitably to draw attention to certain of its more
laughable qualities. But sun and outdoor activity, good cars,

travel, enough but not too much culture, pleasant restaurants, and one's due share of domestic technology and graces are what more businessmen would say make life worth living and constitute a fair reward for their efforts. They are also, if one dares to be frank, what the great majority of their fellow-citizens would like, too, despite all the envious and sour-grapes cries of 'privilege' and 'capitalist perks'. One can ridicule the *New Yorker* advertisements and plenty more in the Sunday newspapers, but the agencies know their business and the values and fantasies they present are by no means pure invention.

REFERENCES

1. *The Director*, January 1965.
2. 'Why Sweden Manages Better', *Management Today*, February 1975.
3. *Britain 1984: a forecast prepared for Unilever*, by Ronald Breck, 1963.
4. 'Industry's Class Divide', *Management Today*, August 1974.
5. *The Director*, May 1969.
6. *Industry in the News*, supplement to *The Director*, January 1963.
7. *The Director*, September 1970.
8. The examples here are taken from the issue of May 26, 1975.

2. The personal reasons for a poor public performance

There is a widespread fear of simple, direct English, yet the inability or the refusal to use straightforward, concrete language is at the root of most failures to get on terms with an audience and to communicate. One might go further than this and say that among many people in positions of responsibility there is a resistance to communicating and a terror of what the results of communication might be. The more meaning one's words contain, the more potentially dangerous they are felt to be.

Thirty years ago two of our most perceptive writers on the state of English, George Orwell[1] and Sir Ernest Gowers,[2] diagnosed and described the disease with admirable accuracy, but neither associated it particularly with business. To Orwell the woolly-minded writers and speakers of nonsense were primarily politicians, especially politicians of the Left, and to Sir Ernest they were Civil Servants. This, however, was before the British industrial scene began to disintegrate and an apparently never-ending series of strikes and so-called industrial disputes, with work brought to a standstill for the most trivial causes, brought out business leaders to a point at which they became inhibited from saying anything definite in public at all, in case it should be seized on and made the occasion of yet another stoppage or bout of wrangling. This neurosis, combined with constant attacks on the right of owners to own, managers to manage and shareholders to receive a return on their money, led, very understandably, to a disastrous fall in confidence, both on the part of individuals and of managers as a group. They no longer believed what they were saying, or felt it necessary to believe what they were saying, and this is a sure recipe for talking nonsense. Some do it more pleasantly or more impressively than others, but, as a transcript reveals all too clearly, it is still nonsense, however much the audience may clap and however kind and obliging journalists may be afterwards. One has communicated only in a negative way; no trouble has followed in the wake of one's words.

The unholy alliance of businessmen, politicians and Civil Servants all under real or imagined pressure to write and speak nonsense has created a kind of automatic style for public occasions which most important people use by instinct. It has, apart from its safety aspect, one great advantage for a busy man; it can be churned out with the utmost ease by hired speech-writers. Since it is anonymous, it is as simple to speak as to write. It is characterised by dead or dying metaphors, pretentious language and meaningless words and phrases. Given a practised performer, it can be produced for an indefinite period and have a soothing and hypnotic effect on an audience, which may even be grateful for not being obliged to make the effort of thinking.

But it is completely irresponsible to leave matters like that. As George Orwell put it so well, the English language 'becomes ugly and inaccurate because our thoughts are foolish, but the slovenliness of our language makes it easier for us to have foolish thoughts'.[3] Improve the language and one improves the thoughts. Direct, concrete language means having real thoughts that mean something. As it is, noted Orwell, 'as soon as certain topics are raised, the concrete melts into the abstract and no one seems able to think of turns of speech that are not hackneyed: prose consists less and less of *words* chosen for the sake of their meaning and more and more of *phrases* tacked together like the sections of a pre-fabricated hen-house.'

If one has something to say, something which exists as a picture in the mind, it becomes normal and human to hunt around for words and images which describe the picture. If, however, there is no firm mental concept, the vacuum has to be filled by a mere string of phrases. Public expression, whether in speech or in writing, consequently consists to a frightening and increasing extent of what Orwell called 'gumming together long strips of words which have already been set in motion by someone else, and making the results presentable by sheer humbug'. But, as he points out, the great attraction of this method of word-spinning – one cannot call it expressing oneself or communicating – is that it is easy. 'It is easier – even quicker, once you have the habit – to say "In my opinion it is a not unjustifiable assumption" than to say "I think". If you use ready-made phrases, you don't have to bother with the rhythms of your sentences, since these phrases are generally so arranged as to be more or less euphonius. When you are composing in a hurry – when you are dictating to a stenographer, for instance, or making a public speech – it is natural to fall into a pretentious, Latinised style. Tags like "a consideration which we should do well to bear in mind", or "a conclusion to which all of us would readily assent" will save many a sentence from coming down with a bump. By using stale metaphors, similes and idioms, you save much mental effort, at the cost of leaving your meaning vague, not only for your reader, but for yourself.'

Now, in the late twentieth century, any effective form of spoken communication – that is, passing a clearly formed thought from the mind of one person to the mind of another and persuading one's listener to react to that thought as one wants him to react – *must* be rooted in an easy, conversational manner. The spirit of the age, as television makes abundantly clear, is against oratory. Unless they are brilliant performers, the platform-politician, the memo-on-two-legs and the Lord-Mayor's-Banquet type of speaker appear merely ridiculous, except, perhaps, to other people who are afflicted in the same way. The rule must be to talk, not to orate.

What does not seem to be widely understood, however, is that a conversational manner is not a second or third-rate manner, and there is certainly no reason for it to be undignified. It is neither necessary nor wise to attempt to grade one's language up for a public occasion. If one makes an effort, consciously or unconsciously, to sound grand or impressive, one is all too likely to collapse or get tied up in knots under pressure. The higher one perches oneself, the further one has to fall. The formula to work to is: clear and well-organised thoughts expressed in one's ordinary, colloquial English. This is in no way a plea for basic English. The occasional technical word or phrase is inevitable, and one should never be afraid to use it, even to a large audience. It is kind and useful to translate or paraphrase it immediately afterwards, however. There is a distinction to be made between technicalities and professional jargon, which is all very well within a closed group, but can be infuriating and baffling to anyone else.

With these general cautions in mind, we can examine a selection of expressions actually used in public, to a general audience, by various people holding responsible positions, who were appearing on behalf of their employers.

'We must,' said the affable general manager of a chemical company, 'take some of the steam out of the candy-floss side of the economy.' It is an agreeable thought, but what, if anything, does it mean to us and what could it have meant to the man who produced it? What was it intended to mean and how did such an absurdly mixed metaphor happen?

'Candy-floss' might be translated as 'enticing frivolities' or 'cheap, appealing luxuries'. 'The candy-floss side of the economy' presumably means, then, that part of the economy which is concerned with the supply and sale of pleasant, showy non-essentials. If one is to 'take some of the steam out of this', one takes away part of its finance and profitability. The statement consequently means something like, 'we must stop investment being frittered away on making and selling cheap and nasty luxuries'. But there is more to 'candy-floss' than this. It also carries the overtones of 'meretricious', 'appealing only to people with an unsophisticated taste', and is consequently a socially-divisive phrase. It can only be used disapprovingly or patronisingly, as a label for the tastes and habits of people who are not sufficiently well-educated to know any better and who are easily taken in by anyone with the skill to exploit their ignorance.

Is this what the man from ICI had in mind? Was he really using 'candy-floss' with any precision at all? Or, as seems much more likely, was he simply putting two clichés together, 'taking steam out' and 'candy-floss', in the vague hope that the results would be impressive? He was, in fact, guilty of the kind of mental laziness which deserves a kick in the bottom rather than a pat on the back. He was not thinking at all, which, for a man with his degree of responsibility and on a public occasion, is a particularly disgraceful form of intellectual treason.

The chairman of a large engineering concern who was asked, on television, what he thought his company's main problem was at that time and replied 'to generate the availability of exposure of our management' would probably have been embarrassed if he had been asked to explain the meaning of such an extraordinary sentence, or if he had been bluntly told that what he had just said was utter nonsense, containing no meaning whatever. Somewhere in the middle of this great lump of managerial cotton-wool there was probably a simple thought, 'we're trying to persuade or compel our managers to make themselves more accessible and better-known to the people they control', but something in the chairman's mind and up-bringing prevented it from coming to the surface in this form. One can almost feel his mental processes at work – 'I must sound dignified, impressive, professional, important. This is a public occasion. The honour of our company is at stake.' But the results of such an effort to impress are so ludicrous that one can only sigh and wonder how young one has to catch executives if they are to be permanently immunised against high-flown rubbish of this kind.

Some years ago *The Times* was obliging enough to publish

the following short letter from the author:

> Sir,
>   Last Friday, in a hotel lobby, I heard one man saying to another: 'UK–Canada link-wise we're production-plus'. Could any of your readers offer a translation? The voice belonged unmistakably to this side of the Atlantic and both men appeared to be about 40.

No suggestions came from readers of *The Times* as to what this remarkable statement might have meant, but it becomes even more extraordinary if one reveals that the conversation took place, not, as delicacy demanded in a letter to *The Times*, in the hotel lobby, but in the hotel lavatories, when even businessmen might reasonably be expected to shed a little of their formality and indulge in rather more relaxed conversation. A hotel lavatory is not, perhaps, a public place in quite the sense that is implied by the title of the present book, but it is difficult to escape the conclusion that something so fundamental had happened to the mind of the man who was production-plus that he would instinctively have said something very similar if he had been taking part in a television interview or speaking at a local flower-show.

One very important, but little discussed reason for this constant and frequently disastrous reaching for the skies in one's language has been an inner need to grade up business itself, so that the perfectly simple, ordinary, useful and occasionally sordid activities of making, buying and selling things shall appear not only reputable but noble. Without some such God-given and God-blessed purpose many businessmen would find it difficult to justify their existence or to continue, or so it appears.

The aims of one very successful company, which 'cares for customers, employees and the public good' are, we have been told in large and correspondingly expensive newspaper advertisements:

1. To be among the most respected companies in the British Commonwealth.
2. To practise new and better methods of commerce.
3. To put principle before expediency and make sure our word is our bond.
4. Whilst not deviating from what is practical to enrol the idealism of youth.
5. To ignore class or race; to judge only by merit; to work in comradeship.
6. To divide more fairly the fruits of investment and work by means of the Mutual Company.
7. To combine what is best in public service, e.g. devotion to duty, with what is best in private enterprise, e.g. adaptability.
8. To express in the tangible terms of guarding and watching Man's regard for his neighbour and wish to serve him.[4]

'Slowly, painfully and persistently', the public has been assured, 'we are climbing to a peak of unimpeachable integrity where service is an end, not just a means.'

Without wishing to deny any company or institution its right to blow its own trumpet from time to time, it is perhaps necessary to remind those who find it possible to write in the holier-than-thou style that certain things, such as keeping to one's word, are better assumed, rather than proclaimed from the house-tops, and that many people nowadays are likely to find the Eight Aims pompous and sentimental, rather than inspiring and crusading. Cynics may well feel impelled to point out that the company in question writes as if it were engaged in a particularly self-sacrificing form of social service, whereas in fact it earns substantial profits from nothing more elevated than guarding factories and offices and shifting van-loads of bank-notes from one part of the country to another. This, however, is not the point we are trying to make. Our present interest in the public pronouncements of this perfectly respectable and useful company and of a number of other large organisations lies in the fact that they are an attempt to turn mutton into lamb, if not caviare, and that their prose-poem style encourages other businessmen to consider simple, concrete, colloquial language inferior and even low. In this sense, such advertisements have a corrupting, cloying effect. Individual businessmen feel a pressure, sometimes, no doubt, a sub-conscious pressure, to use them as models for their own public utterances.

'Tiptoe on the misty mountain tops', says the Morgan Crucible Company, in the summary of its 1974 Annual Report.[5] 'We would never have scaled the profit peak of 1974 without the whole-hearted co-operation of all our people throughout the world. There are further peaks in the mountain range to be scaled but, given the present state of world trade, we will certainly pause for breath in 1975. Even the chamois must on occasion stop before again leaping upward. Although it is hard to see through the swirling mists of the immediate future, it remains as true as ever that Morgan is uniquely placed to take advantage of any general economic revival, and more particularly the accelerating demand for energy conservation in the developed world and for basic industrialisation in the developing world; poised, like the chamois, for the next sure-footed leap upwards.'

After a little of this, it is tempting to ask one or two people what remains in their mind. What do they remember of the golden words that have been put in the Chairman's mouth? The answer, almost certainly, is 'exceedingly little'. The language has a certain hypnotic effect. One is carried along by a feeling of dazed respect, in which the basic message, '1975 is going to be a stagnant year', is likely to find itself quietly and decently buried. The whole passage is a clever confidence trick, with chamois-leaps suggesting a degree of energy and forward movement which is not really there at all.

This, however, displays a high degree of skill. It is a professional job. Those businessmen who try to pitch their remarks at what they feel to be the same level are more likely to achieve cliché and dullness than hypnosis. Here are some examples from talks and interviews given by business executives of the deadening results of a refusal to use plain, conversational English.

As spoken	*Translated*
'There is a shortage of bed-space in the Metropolis'	It's difficult to find a hotel room in London
'Financially, if things were favourable, I would retire'	If I had enough money, I'd retire
'On initial arrival at the hotel'	When we got to the hotel
'Basically, we are endeavouring to . . .'	We're trying to . . .
'People who have generally resided in a quiet neighbourhood'	People who've generally lived in a quiet district
'We endeavour to render humanitarian service'	We're trying to save lives
'We aim at buyer-satisfaction'	We want people who buy our goods to be satisfied
'We despatched an inspector'	We sent an inspector
'The conversion operation is of limited duration'	It doesn't take long to convert your equipment
'Our company purchases apples'	Our company buys apples
'Salaries are much more lucrative'	Salaries are higher
'We shall review the validity of the maps'	We'll check to make sure the maps are up-to-date
'Prior to December last year'	Until last December

It is not unknown for people who have used the sentence or phrase given in the first column to challenge the translation provided in the second. To 'purchase apples', or to 'acquire a factory', they say, is not the same as to 'buy apples', or 'buy a factory'. This is an interesting phenomenon and it is worth devoting a few moments to an attempt to understand it. To the manager of a cider factory, 'purchasing apples' is a large-scale activity, involving hundreds or thousands of tons, whereas anyone who goes into a greengrocer's shop 'buys' a pound of apples. An industrial concern, for the same reason, speaks of its 'purchasing officer', not 'buying officer', although, curiously enough one large retail concern, Marks and Spencer, employs 'buyers', not 'purchasers'. In most instances, then, 'purchasing' is considered more professional than mere 'buying', and to say 'buy', instead of 'purchase', is to run a serious risk of losing status and of not being able to justify one's salary. In the same way, to 'buy a factory' suggests a much smaller and less worthwhile operation than to 'acquire a factory'.

One can dismiss this kind of attitude as childish and refuse to show any sympathy with it, but that is not a very constructive approach. Status is a matter of great importance in industry and it has to be reflected, both on the management and on the Trade Union side, by a careful use of the appropriate language. Within an industry or a firm, this may be all very well, but when an industrialist or a Trade Union leader has to present himself to the big world instead of to his familiar little world, his status means nothing. He is naked, with only his merits as an individual to carry him through. The fact that he is an apple-purchaser, rather than an apple-buyer, is of absolutely no significance at all and, if he wilfully persists in purchasing, he will merely appear pompous, unnatural and anxious to cut himself off from his fellow-men.

A curious failure to realise this occurred during 1974, the person involved being a high-ranking official of one of the regional gas boards. This gentleman, in his late fifties, was very conscious of his rank and dignity. One of his most important tasks, he said, was to 'motivate' his staff. Invited to explain what he meant by 'motivate', he became angry and insisted that there was no other word to convey what he had in mind. After a few minutes of persistent prodding, the interview succeeded in producing an explosion, which threw up a memorable definition of this difficult word. It meant, said the Regional Controller, 'persuading the buggers to work harder, even when no one was watching them', but this was, even so, not the same in his opinion as 'motivate', which was a professional term for a professional function.

Professional managers, like any other kind of professional, owe much of their success and prestige to the specialised language with which they surround themselves. The fact that this is either incomprehensible or only half comprehensible to the lay world allows them to surround themselves with a mystique which they feel, rightly or wrongly, acts to their advantage. To be asked to drop this special phraseology and the habit of mind on which it depends is, for some people, to deprive them of much of their personality, and they resist it very hard.

But it is not only the use of incomprehensible language which cuts someone off from the bulk of his audience and makes communication difficult. How one speaks is of just as much importance as what one speaks, and there can be no arguing about the fact that for any speaker, businessman or not, on any occasion, the most important quality is energy. Given energy, one can get away with almost anything; without it, one's faults and blemishes are almost all the audience has to be interested in. There are, however, two quite distinct types of energy. One is controlled, a musician's energy, punching what needs to be punched and withdrawing gently and quickly from what deserves reflexion or what is no more than in-filling. This kind of energy follows the sense of what is being said and makes for understanding. The second and, alas, more frequent type is bogus energy, the flat-out energy of the sports commentator, the average television and radio reporter, the high-pressure salesman. The person armed with this kind of isn't-everything-marvellous-and-exciting energy aims at stunning the people who are listening to him and sweeping them along exhausted and in a trance in the direction he wants them to go. They are not to be given a chance to discriminate between one piece of information and another, since reflexion might, and probably would break the spell. A transcript of this type of energetic talk would certainly look dreadful. No-one in their right mind sets a boxing commentary or a description of the Derby on paper.

An interesting point to notice about the flat-out people is

that they rarely use their hands to emphasise and accompany what they are saying. They are, with rare exceptions, purely voice-men. There is an important reason for this. Anyone who is accustomed to using his hands a great deal when he talks is communicating with his body quite as much as with his voice. He is, so to speak, conducting his own orchestra and, without thinking about the matter at all, his hands and movements will follow the sense of what he is saying. The important words and syllables will be marked by a strong beat from the hands and because, physically, the speaker feels they are important, these meaning-carrying sounds will be pushed harder. The brain tells the hands what to do and the hands help the voice to perform more efficiently. The point is so obvious in most countries of the world that in, say, France or Italy, it would seem hardly worth making, but in Britain, where to gesticulate is to be guilty of highly suspect and downright Latin behaviour, the truth of it has to be driven in with a sledge-hammer, especially at the managerial levels of society. Nothing is more likely to put life into a dull speaker than the simple trick of allowing one's hands to move freely.

Many people, especially those who have risen from the ranks – the first-generation executives – are worried about their accents, sometimes to the point of neurosis. This is hardly surprising, in view of the traditional public-school background of British directors, which we have already documented. The surest way to arrive is to look and sound like the people who are already there, as ambitious men have realised for generations. As one exceptional bishop once remarked to the author, 'I can't understand how I ever came to be a bishop. I didn't go to a public school, or to Oxford or Cambridge, and I don't sound like the other people on the Bench of Bishops.' Some men – Mr Roy Jenkins is an excellent example – achieve miracles in their deliberate attempts to lose one accent and acquire another. Mr Jenkins, whose South Wales origins are very recent, has even added to his public equipment that ultimate badge of upper-class refinement, the half-pronounced R, known to connoisseurs in

Britain at one time as the Third Programme R and now, since organisational changes in the BBC, as the Radio 3 R. His well-deserved success in the Army, in commerce and in politics suggests that determination and a good ear can pay off.

It may be, however, that Mr Jenkins' generation will be the last to benefit from this kind of veneer, although, even during the past quarter of a century its usefulness has varied very much from industry to industry and from career to career. The traditional upper-class accent has undoubtedly been a great help, if not absolutely essential, to anyone with ambitions in, for instance, brewing, merchant banking, stockbroking, publishing or the law, although here, too, things have been changing. The board of Allied Breweries, a company which has disturbed the brewing industry in a number of ways, contains more than one owner of a non-U[6] accent, yet its chairman, Mr Keith Showering, is not one of them, despite his Babycham upbringing. The Showering family, for thirty years the leading citizens of the small Somerset town of Shepton Mallet, and its principal benefactors, have, with this one exception, remained in appearance, speech and manner, the solid yeomen cidermakers their ancestors always were. The phenomenal post-war success of their great fruit-juice invention, Babycham, made them millionaires. To have had a Babycham upbringing, as Mr Keith Showering did, is to be counted among the most favoured children of British industry. A distinctly fruity, club-man variety of the public-school accent is normal at the upper levels of one company in the Allied Breweries group, Harveys, where this kind of manner and sound is presumably reckoned to help in projecting the correct image of the wines the company sells.

A Scottish accent creates no problems anywhere, partly because, for some unexplained reason, it suggests honesty and trustworthiness, and partly because few people outside Scotland can place it socially. To those who are not Welsh, a Welsh accent may sound comic, but, fortunately for those who possess it, almost never dull. Lancashire and Yorkshire may also have too many echoes of music-hall comedians to allow the people who wear these accents to be taken entirely seriously, especially in the South, but just a touch of them can give an impression of solid democratic worth. So, too, can a dash of West Country. More than a dash gives rise to thoughts of cows, cider and bucolic idleness, shading off into Acker Bilk-like rusticity.

The most difficult accent to carry in Britain, since the Beatles made Liverpudlian respectable, is almost certainly the one that belongs to the Birmingham area. Flat, unmusical and redolent of foundries and car-assembly lines, it probably causes more anxieties and regrets than any other. The speech characteristics of London and the South-East cause less trouble, soul-searching and apologies nowadays than they used to before the Second World War. Middle-class Londoners prefer that their children should not acquire Cockney dipthongs, which are extremely hard to get rid of later in life, and people in other parts of Britain often think Londoners are rude and abrupt. French provincials have a similar attitude to Parisians. Life in any metropolis tends to nip the niceties and graces of life in the bud, and the local accent and intonation shows it. New Yorkers have a similar reputation for regarding words as valuable commodities, to be handed out with a proper sense of economy and without wasting time on the luxury of politeness. The reputation of different accents in the United States is of considerable social importance, although not in quite the same way as in Britain. Well-to-do American women set much store on looking and sounding 'refined' – they will, for example, take great pains to wear washed-out pastel shades in order not to be confused with negroes and hippies who go boldly for the bright colours – but the effect, to a European, is not always what the ladies concerned might have hoped. Fortunately for the Americans, perhaps, there is nothing in America which corresponds to U-speech in Britain. Among elderly people, there is still a certain amount of prestige attached to a New England accent, especially of the Boston-Harvard variety, but it comes in for a good deal of ridicule from the young, and, on the whole, the sun-echoing, new-life-reflecting accent and intonation of California are the most highly regarded nowadays. It should go without saying, of course, that Americans are as quick as any other people to recognise an educated person from his speech and that any idea that social and educational differences are not reflected in the way Americans talk is ludicrous.

At this point one should emphasise with all possible firmness that since the 1939–45 war, and to some extent as a result of it, the technical man has come into his kingdom in Britain, and that technical men have a way of sounding very different from the Oxbridge, humanities-trained men who preceded them as managers. A high proportion of them come from the industrial areas of Britain, not from the shires and the gentler South, and a great many were reared in working-class and lower middle-class households. As a consequence of this, the traditional educated English accent has long since ceased to predominate, at least in those industries where technical men abound and have power. Lunch in the executive dining room at any ICI works, or at the company's headquarters at Millbank, will reveal a fine range of Scottish and Northern accents. So, too, will a visit to Ford, British Leyland, or any steelworks. But, in almost any court of law, whether in London or elsewhere, one will have to listen very hard to catch a Northern or Midland accent among the barristers or judges.

One could usefully round off this brief disquisition on accents by mentioning the story of the Midlands manager of a large national concern who had ambitions to rise fast and far in the organisation. Aged 35, he had a marked Australian accent. Asked about this when on a course, he admitted that he had never been to Australia in his life. He had noticed some years previously, however, that the power-group at headquarters had that special blend of military and public school in their voices which marked them off as destined to hold the top jobs and which, to anyone coming late to the task, is very difficult to acquire. If one had not got at least the basis of it by the time one is fourteen, it is best to forget about it. Faced with this unwelcome barrier to advancement, our hero, whose own upbringing had been in Wolverhampton, decided to abandon all English accents and to go Australian, on the very reasonable grounds that nobody would be likely to object to having a bright Australian on the Board, although they might well turn up their noses at Wolverhampton. By diligent application and a remarkable degree of self-discipline, he had got rid of his old shell entirely and he was now as Australian as if he had spent his entire life in Sydney. Nobody, including his own employers, could label him socially, or educationally. He was classless, rootless and safe. There are Englishmen who have achieved the same results by turning themselves into Americans, which works satisfactorily in some occupations, but would not have been acceptable in this very British organisation.

It is a sad fact that a great many people holding very responsible positions in Britain are apparently unable to understand that there are important differences between written and spoken English, and that to speak like a company memo is disastrous. One could go further and say that a considerable proportion of our business leaders are little more than memos on two legs. Ask them a question and part of a memo, sometimes the whole document, comes back in reply.

This is not merely a matter of house-jargon, although anyone who can bring himself to declare in public, as the Director of Engineering of one of the Regional Gas Boards did, that 'the average domestic consumer is temperature-sensitive' clearly has his work in his bones. It applies much more to sentence structure and to contractions. The General Manager of one of the Post Office's major telephone areas, a man who had grown up with the Post Office and, if he and his employers will pardon the term, sounded like it, was quite unable to hear any difference between

'It is nice to have a telephone'
which he had said, and

'It's nice to have a telephone',

which was what one was trying to persuade him to say. Similarly, he could not distinguish between 'any alterations they have made' and 'any alterations they've made'. It was useless to point out to him that, if he were to spend a little time listening to the ordinary conversation of his fellow citizens, of whatever class or background, he would hear them saying 'It's terrible weather, isn't it', not 'It is terrible weather, is it not'. Nor did one make much progress by suggesting that, in this respect, he himself was no different from the man in the street or the man in the works canteen, and that the betting was at least a thousand to one that he would bark at his wife, 'Aren't you ready yet?', not 'Are you not ready yet?'

The block in his mind was a fear of sounding low and not up to the occasion. To anyone who feels like this, colloquialisms – and normal contractions are thought of as colloquialisms – are not appropriate when one has to make any kind of public statement. In extreme cases, such as the one we have just mentioned, conditioning to this attitude is so complete that the contracted form is literally unthinkable. It is not heard for what it is, even when it is presented as a possible alternative.

This is a great nuisance and a very serious barrier to easy, effective communication, but it is deep-rooted and for that reason difficult to remove. It is particularly common among men who left school early and whose education has never been equal to their talents, and, regrettably, among women of all ages and educational backgrounds. Broadly speaking, we could say that half-educated men are terrified of sounding uneducated and that most women are equally terrified of being thought unladylike. In both instances, colloquialisms are felt to drag one down to the level of the herd, when the fact that one is speaking in public and quite possibly being broadcast is evidence that one is a superior, selected person.

This very ill-informed view is widely encouraged, alas, by many people who ought to know better, not least television and radio producers. Listen, for instance, to any reading or dramatisation of one of Jane Austen's novels. For some extraordinary reason, the characters are made to speak, consistently, dialogue of the 'It is a pity it is raining this morning, is it not?' type, although there is absolutely no evidence that even the grandest and most elegant of the Georgians or Victorians talked like this. They said, exactly as we do, 'It's a pity it's raining this morning, isn't it?' Jane Austen, however, observed the normal literary convention of writing out all these forms in full, and the printer naturally followed suit. So, too, did Trollope's printer, Thackeray's printer and the printer of every other nineteenth century novel of manners and social life.

Nowadays, perhaps understandably, these novels and the plays that were contemporary with them are felt to come from a Golden Age of English, when the language was spoken and written 'properly', with a precision and an attention to detail that will never be seen again, an age when everything was under control and when people of breeding and property ruled the country. In our own times, the Queen, in her broadcasts and speeches, obligingly continues what might as well be called the Jane Austen tradition, although the attribution is not at all fair to Jane Austen. The Queen says, as one might expect of someone in such an exalted position, 'We cannot think', instead of 'we can't think', and provides a powerful prop for the anti-contractors. But it is no great help to more ordinary mortals, who have to live and work within the current idioms.

There is, even so, more to spoken English than contractions. One of its most distinctive features is that it moves along in a more or less straight line, with signals and items of information set out as a chain, linked and divided by full stops, 'ands' and 'buts'. The ear can pass on information to the brain most easily and conveniently this way, by taking in material one bit at a time and in a logical sequence. A listener follows a speaker best when his material is presented in this form.

I was coming along the road yesterday morning and there,

on the corner, was an ice-cream van. Four children rushed
out of their front gates and one of them was nearly killed
by a car that went by much too fast, just as he stepped off the
pavement.

Brick is added methodically and sensibly to brick and the
listener can cope. This, however, is quite another matter:

> I'd just left my house the other morning – it's a semi-detached
> house, with a long path up to the front door and quite a lot of
> shrubs and trees so that you don't really notice the length of
> the garden – and I was coming down the road which goes to
> the station and passes a butcher's shop on the right-hand side,
> and there, on the corner, where Mr Jones lives, was an ice-
> cream van, which, in all probability, had just stopped. Four
> children – I suppose the eldest would have been about ten
> and the youngest maybe four – rushed out of their front gates,
> and one of them, a boy, as you might have supposed, was
> nearly killed – my heart was in my mouth, as you can well
> imagine – by a car that went by just as he stepped off the
> pavement and without giving me any chance to take its
> number.

The second example does not proceed unswervingly in a
straight line. It steps frequently to one side or another, qualifying what has been said, slipping in an explanation or a
second thought. These sidesteps are clearly indicated in
print by words like 'which', 'as' and 'so', and by hyphens.
The story is told in a series of ballet movements, instead of
a straightforward march, and the listener, unlike the reader,
can be forgiven if he gets lost from time to time and takes a
while to get back on course.

Relatives – who, which – are very little used in spoken
English, and anyone who builds them into the framework
of his sentences is liable to be thought odd or stuck-up. 'The
point I was trying to make' disturbs nobody, but 'The point
which I was trying to make' sounds unmistakably written, not
spoken. So, too, does 'also', which, to many people's surprise,
is not a conversational word.

To use the impersonal pronoun, 'one', as in 'One would

hardly think so', or 'He's not a man one would trust' is to be labelled as belonging to a small minority group. Not more than five per cent of people in Britain are one-people, which is in some ways a pity, because an impersonal pronoun, properly used, is a useful thing for any language to have. 'You would hardly think so', or 'People would hardly think so' are no clearer, more forceful or even more democratic than 'One would hardly think so', but it is possible to have too much of a good thing. Heavy users of 'one', such as Princess Anne, and, no doubt, the members of the circle within which she moves, sound very ridiculous indeed to those who observe the habit as laymen and from outside. The great crime and the principal absurdity is to say 'one' as an alternative to 'I'. There is no need to dwell on Princess Anne's apocryphal 'One will' in her marriage service, but it makes the point. 'One' can be not only a fashionable, but also a cowardly and dishonest way of remaining a shadowy figure in the background and of refusing to answer questions directly and personally. 'Are you satisfied with the way the new model's selling?' deserves either 'Yes, I'm very satisfied' or 'I don't think it's going too badly', or 'No, I'm not very satisfied', not 'One could say it isn't going too badly'. An audience wakes up and pays attention when it hears 'I', but 'one' sends it to sleep.

An actual example will show the close inter-relationship of a number of the points made so far in this chapter. The problem was, on the face of it, a fairly simple one. The Market Research Manager of one of our biggest cigarette companies was worried about his repeated failure to make an impact at conferences and conventions called to launch a new line or to inspire the retail trade or his own colleagues with confidence, or to explain some change in marketing policy. Did he work from a script, he was asked, or from notes, or perhaps he looked his audience straight in the eye and did the whole thing extempore? There was always, it emerged, a full script; the Board would never permit any other method. Every word and comma had to be approved in advance and the script had to be delivered exactly as it was typed, in its final agreed version. We asked to see a sample script and persuaded the Market Research Manager to read it. Immediately the nature of the problem became clear. The unfortunate man had been given an impossible task.

In the extract which follows only those changes have been made which would allow the company to be identified. The talk, it should be explained, was accompanied and illustrated by slides, and the script contained instructions as to when the picture was to change. 'Slide 12 off, slide 13 on', the procedure was laid down to the second.

This was part of the page of script, as officially approved and delivered.

> Finally a look at the King Size market. This section constantly moves against the pattern one intuitively feels it ought to follow, in the face of economic reality. Although King Size brands react sensitively to price increases in the short run, they have proved more resilient over time than the B class brands, and the Class now accounts for $6\frac{1}{2}$ per cent, compared with only 5 per cent in 1968. The King Size market continues to be dominated by the Smith and Jolliffe King Size which currently accounts for almost half the class. Neither of the other two main brands in the Class, Griddle's King Size and Sir John Falstaff, appear able to make any impression on the continued dominance of Smith and Jolliffe.

Everything about this suggests part of an article or a memorandum, not a talk. It purports to be written for speaking, but it is not in spoken English. Nobody – not even a Marketing Research Manager, who must breathe as much professional jargon in the course of a working day as anyone in the country – would ever *say* during conversation, things like 'has begun to decline in response to economic pressures', or 'make any impression on the continued dominance of'.

We made an attempt to translate it into something closer to spoken English, with this result:

> And now to round off this survey of what's happening, let's have a look at the King Size market. There's an interesting and rather curious thing about this market. It will persist in

moving against the pattern one feels it ought to follow, or
perhaps I should say, the pattern an economist feels it ought
to follow. King Size brands do certainly react pretty sensitively
to price increases in the short term but, over a longer period,
they've been more resilient than the B class brands. This class
now has $6\frac{1}{2}$ per cent of the market, compared with only
5 per cent in 1968.

The King Size market's still led by Smith and Jolliffe.
They've got nearly half of it. Neither of the other two main
brands, Griddle's King Size and Sir John Falstaff, seem to
be able to do anything about it. Smith and Jolliffe stay right
on top.

Even so, Maharajah's here, it completes our Princes range
and I'm sure it's won over a lot of Princes smokers who were
looking for something different at the weekend or for special
occasions.

Our Marketing Manager put this across quite easily. It felt,
he said, 'completely different'. We set out the differences for
him, in the hope that he might find it possible to pass them
on to higher authority. First, we pointed out, we had got rid
of all the words and phrases that we couldn't imagine him
using in a conversation with his colleagues. Then we had
shortened and restructured most of the sentences, to give
him a chance to make the pauses and emphases that would
allow points to be pushed home easily. And, finally, we had
made sure that all the pronoun and verb combinations were
typed in their contracted forms *on the typescript*, to stop him
falling back into his old bad habits.

In the process of working all this out and applying it, this
particular executive revealed certain dramatic gifts which he
had previously given us no reason to suspect. They had, in
fact, been temporarily suppressed by the appallingly bad
committee text – all committee texts are bad, but some are
worse than others – which he had been forced to try to put
across.

Good actors are not common among businessmen at the
highest levels, mainly, one suspects, because most of them
are frightened of making fools of themselves and of losing

their dignity, a protective shell which they value very highly. It is equally rare to find, in any country, top men in any commercial or industrial organisation who have a strong sense of humour. This does not go with the breed. Well below the top, it is not uncommon, although it is usually an effective barrier to any further progress, since men who are able to laugh at themselves and at life are unlikely to have the necessary degree of single-mindedness to carry them to the ultimate positions of power. There is nothing to be done about this.

One's physical appearance is a much less serious obstacle to a successful public performance than most of the other matters that have been discussed above. Gross defects, such as a cleft-lip, a large scar or a missing nose or ear are unhelpful, especially on television, mainly because an audience devotes so much attention to studying them that there is little left over for what the speaker is trying to say. But anything less than this can be handled without too much trouble, unless the speaker should happen to have a face which recalls that of some well-known and ill-liked person of eminence. At various times it has not benefitted a man to bear a close resemblance to, say, Adolf Hitler, Neville Chamberlain, Ronald Biggs, the Great Train Robber, or anyone else urgently wanted by the police. It is not easy, either, for an audience to ignore the fact that a leader of industry is strangely like a well-known actor. It is a wise man who knows his double, especially when the double is much better known than oneself.

It is a great handicap for an ambitious businessman to have fair hair. With fair hair, one can do well enough in publishing, medicine or the Civil Service, but it is the very exceptional man who completely overcomes the disadvantage in the worlds of manufacturing, finance and commerce, where the prejudice in favour of dark-haired or one-time dark-haired men is strongly marked, although discussion of the matter is semi-taboo. For some totally illogical reason, the public, like employers, seems unwilling to include fair hair in the business stereotype. On television, as in front of a selection board, the fair-haired man starts with a disadvantage, which he has to work hard at to overcome.

But there is no need to develop a neurosis about such matters. The all-important thing is to develop a style and a manner of dressing that suits one's appearance, and to be aware of the aspects of one's appearance that are likely or certain to catch the attention of an audience. Unusual height or fatness, splendidly huge eyebrows, very deep-set eyes, an Adam's apple of striking size, a skull with little flesh or hair on it, all these are characteristics which seize the fancy of the people one is looking at and talking to and which need a little time to digest. Until one's appearance has been, so to speak, accepted by an audience, it is a waste of time to try to communicate any great thought.

NOTES AND REFERENCES

1. 'Politics and the English Language'. Originally published in *Horizon*, April 1946. Reprinted in *The Collected Essays, Journalism and Letters of George Orwell*, Vol. 4, 1968.
2. *Plain Words*, 1948.
3. *Politics and the English Language*.
4. *The Times*, October 22, 1971.
5. *The Times*, July 1, 1975.
6. U and non-U are necessary equipment for anyone travelling through the jungle of English social life. They indicate, broadly speaking, that a person either does (U) or does not (non-U) belong to the best-bred, most fashionably educated, best-connected sector of society and that one possesses or does not possess the special speech-habits and other vitally important tribal customs which immediately reveal to an initiate whether the person one is speaking to is worth meeting again or not. It is a situation which no foreigner can hope to cope with and the attempt is a waste of energy.

3. The social reasons for a poor public performance

'For the man on the way up,' says a circular from the Business Leaders' Book Club, 'business life is a rat race' For every success you achieve there are a dozen people, or circumstances over which you may have no control, waiting to snatch what you have gained. And every single year, colleges turn out more graduates who have learned the latest techniques of getting ahead – many of which didn't even exist as little as five years ago. That is why, business being so competitive, you must seize every opportunity to advance and secure your position.'

The picture is not a pleasant one, but it comes close to the reality of many people's lives. What the Business Leaders' Book Club is saying amounts to this. There are only 24 hours in the day and, however bright and vigorous you may be, you have only a limited amount of energy. All your time and all your energy must be devoted to doing your job better than anybody else can, keeping abreast of the latest business methods, playing business politics and cultivating the people who are likely to be useful to you. This is what getting on means. There will be very little of you to spare for your family, for relaxation, for broadening your mind or deepening your personal culture. These things are luxuries that only non-ambitious people can afford to indulge in. They are not for you.

And so we have the eternal round of business lunches, business dinners, lodge meetings, cocktail parties and maybe golf, although the amount of use that non-American businessmen make of the golf club and as a social centre is probably not very great nowadays. In the professions, the situation is not usually as bad. Doctors do not spend nearly all their leisure-time with other doctors or lawyers with other lawyers and, in any case, their work necessarily brings them into contact with a wide range of people. Politicians, however, see far too much of other politicians, and come to believe as a result that everyone finds politics as absorbing as they do. Civil servants tend not to spend their free time cultivating other civil servants, partly because their promotion chances are not likely to be greatly increased that way, and partly because the tradition of business eating and drinking is not, as yet, very highly developed among them.

Those members of the business community who have to work closely with the public – salesmen, bank clerks, tax officers are examples which come readily to mind – have plenty of opportunity to meet their fellow citizens and, at least in theory, to listen to their opinions and ways of expressing themselves. In practice, however, most of this type of communication is of a very restricted kind. An employee of a large store may learn a good deal about the public's tastes and requirements in dress materials, tinned soup or cookers, but he or she is unlikely to gain valuable information about his customers' feelings concerning the Middle East situation, the state of the stock market or the pollution of rivers. The odd revealing remark may hit him from time to time, but, in general, what comes his way will be fairly pedestrian stuff.

As he moves up the ladder – if he moves up the ladder – even these potentially humanising influences are likely to be removed from him, and a large part of the company he keeps will be composed of people like himself, talking the same language as he does and living life to the same pattern. If he has any heretical or eccentric thoughts, he will have learnt long ago to keep them to himself, conscious all the while of how vulnerable and expendable he is in a system which would like, if it could, to employ only a constant succession of young men. A few years ago a certain internationally known electronics concern held a prestigious reception at the Dorchester Hotel in London, to launch a new model in one of its lines of equipment. The employees of the company were distinguished from the visitors and prospective customers by means of somewhat aggressive button-hole badges, and their youth was obvious. Half-way through the day, the present author found an occasion to speak to the company's Managing Director, a very heavy, coarse and notoriously ruthless individual, and put this question to him, 'Don't you have anybody on the payroll, except for yourself, who's over 35?' His answer summed up the current philosophy of large-scale capitalist industry in what is quite possibly its final, backs-to-the-wall stage, 'We do our best not to.' Not all managing directors would have been so honest.

At another conference, this time arranged by a university to discuss the problem of retraining and resettling managerial and technical staff whom Fate and economic change have made redundant, one of those attending was the head of the personnel department of a large, science-based British concern. Asked why he was there, he replied, in the most simple and direct terms, 'To discover how the good employer can get rid of 500 graduate scientists as painlessly as possible'.

Redundancy and the constant pressure of younger, fresher men coming up from below are unlikely to discourage a tendency to conform. The more difficult it becomes to find and hold a job suited to one's abilities, the less probable it is that people holding important positions will feel inclined to adopt bold postures and put forward original ideas. This, in theory, should not happen, at least to the same extent, in the nationalised industries and in central and local government, where security of tenure is almost absolute, where idleness and inefficiency are no barrier to continued employment, and where a man or woman has almost to commit a criminal offence in order to find himself out of a job. Public servants, however, have a tradition, admirable in many circumstances, of keeping their mouths shut and, on those rare occasions when they cannot avoid saying something in public, of confining themselves to tactful generalities. This is not an age of fearless statements, mainly because such a high proportion of the people with executive responsibility are themselves paralysed and emasculated by fear of one thing or another – fear of dismissal or non-promotion, fear of strikes, fear of intrigue, fear of falling sales and bankruptcy. Everyone, to a greater or lesser extent, is looking over his shoulder every time he opens his mouth, and this makes it more and more difficult to achieve a brilliant or memorable public performance. Good speaking and good writing can only come from confident people who are not afraid to express their real thoughts. Any civilisation gets the level of communication it deserves.

But confidence is relative and it can depend very much on the subject about which one is speaking. A businessman can be a woolly, unconvincing idiot when he is talking about the problems of his business, but splendidly interesting on football or dogs. A senior civil servant or a cabinet minister may produce little solid information or sparkle if he is addressing an audience on some theme connected with his work, but the same man is not infrequently excellent in a talk on old silver, the history of the Oxford and Cambridge Boat Race or the growing of carnations. The moral is clear: the good performance comes from the person who, on that occasion at least, feels free and an individual.

A few companies go to considerable trouble to make sure that their senior staff do have regular opportunities to meet a cross-section of interesting people from completely different walks of life. One or two of the banks manage this very well and so do some of the bigger stockbroking firms and retailing groups. Newspapers entertain influential people methodically and as a matter of course. In general, however, business sees guests mainly as people to be softened up, placated and influenced, rather than as carriers of useful and stimulating ideas, and when outsiders do come to lunch or dinner the people from the company who are given the chance to meet them are, in nine cases out of ten, executives within a few years of retirement, rather than younger men on whom the benefit of a breath of fresh air from time to time would be more marked.

Before it was absorbed out of existence by Barclays, Martin's Bank followed a refreshingly enlightened policy of what is known in the trade as staff-enrichment. Apart from employing exceptionally good architects to design and furnish their buildings up and down the country, and giving local managers an opportunity to discuss ideas with them, which for the most part was an introduction to a completely new language and outlook on life, Martin's regional managers were encouraged to organise fortnightly lunches, in private dining rooms which were a pleasure in themselves, so that for two hours a couple of members of the staff could exchange ideas in complete privacy with four people who worked within the particular region or who happened to be visiting it at the time. A typical quartet might include the manager of the local repertory theatre, a professor of history, the captain of the county cricket team and the editor of the woman's page on the city's evening paper. The talk flowed, the bank made good friends and, most important of all, for two hours a couple of future general managers learnt to handle other people's language and to adapt their own to it.

This kind of exercise should form part of the training of every executive, not once a year or when the whim happens to take the managing director, but regularly and frequently. One notices, with a sigh, that such activities are much more likely to take place when the man in charge is himself a person of broad general culture and wide interests, as indeed he should be, but, in Britain, all too seldom is. However successful he may have been in crude professional or commercial terms, no top executive is going to expose his ignorance, willingly and at his company's expense, to outsiders who might have preferred to lunch with someone less narrow in his experience and mental equipment. It is not an accident that those concerns, which for many years have made a special point of attracting, and keeping, exceptionally well-educated and mentally curious people to their managerial staff, also have the best record of success in the cross-fertilisation of ideas between their own employees and men and women from quite different fields. The founder of that great English retailing institution, the John Lewis Partnership, the redoubtable John Spedan Lewis, went so far, indeed, as to recruit to his staff, at high salaries, people like admirals, professors of English literature and eminent lawyers, on the grounds that they helped, despite their total ignorance of the drapery trade, to keep the minds of his professional managers open and alert.

One cannot, of course, expect everyone to be interested in everything, but it is remarkable how many high-ranking executives one meets, from generals to the heads of insurance companies and from the managers of large hotels to men running airlines, who appear to have no serious interests outside their job whatever, who never read books and who, on matters away from their field of professional competence, have the prejudices and stock of information of people many layers below them in intelligence and income. Unless one is willing to confine one's remarks to their job, sport, cars, sex, inflation or the weather, it is literally impossible to hold a conversation with them, and with their wives it is often much worse, since the majority of them have only their husband's job to talk about, not their own.

It is easy to excuse them by saying that it is not their fault, and to a large extent this is true. British society in particular makes it difficult to bandy ideas about with strangers. To introduce a serious note into a conversation is to render oneself immediately suspect, unless the parties concerned know one another well and the occasion is very private. To be an intellectual in Britain is, it has been well said, a black market activity, in a way that it is not abroad, except perhaps in Australia, where the situation is even worse than it is in Britain.

It is necessary, however, to make a clear distinction between what one knows and what one says. To make a parade of one's knowledge is vulgar and boring, but to have a well-filled mind available in case of need is another matter entirely. At the

moment we are talking about the second and our lament is
that so many businessmen in the English-speaking world do
not, from the evidence they provide, have well-filled minds
and for that reason they are all-too frequently at a loss on
occasions when a well-filled mind is an essential tool. Some of
the blame for this should certainly be laid at the door of their
employers, for creating the impression that work and getting
on are the gods to which everything else should be sacrificed,
but the people directly involved can hardly be held blameless
for being content and even eager to accept such a situation,
year after year. It would be ridiculous to suggest that everybody in a post of high responsibility has got there by devoting
every minute of his working life to satisfying his ambition and
that he is totally uncultured and ill-read as a result. This is
certainly not true and anyone who moves about in the business
world could produce a list of very different men at the other
end of the spectrum. But there are too many uncultured
people in positions of power for our national comfort and this
is a situation which should worry all of us. If the disease of the
British working-classes is a proneness to go on strike at the
drop of a hat, the disease of the managerial classes is low tastes
in high places, and this goes, alas, for politicians just as much
as for businessmen.

In one's working life it is possible to get by and even to
prosper with a very poor command of English. The assumption is too readily made that because someone has been born
and bred in England he will necessarily be able to handle his
mother tongue. This is true, in the sense that he is unlikely to
be mistaken for a foreigner. He will be able to talk fluently and
idiomatically, give orders and swear in the correct English
way. What he is extremely unlikely to be able to do, if he has
not read good authors and taken part in good conversation, is
to handle the full resources of the language with confidence
and discrimination. And unless he can do this, he will inevitably remain a poor speaker, no matter what the advertisements
for the more unscrupulous speaking courses may tell him.
Shades of meaning and subtleties will pass him by, references

will escape him and irony and understatement will be lost on
him. He will be a cultural and linguistic cripple, and such a
man can be very painful to listen to.

If one's vocabulary is poor, as it almost inevitably will be
if one has never come into contact with writers and talkers
who use words well, there are many things which one cannot
say or understand. To express one's own emotions even
adequately and to be sensitive to those of others demands a
rich and well-exercised vocabulary, and it is on the emotive
use of language that businessmen, practical men, money-
making men, power-happy men most frequently fall down.
They tend to be good on facts, poor on feelings, which is
another way of saying that they have received only the flattest,
dullest and most pedestrian part of their linguistic and cultural
inheritance. They have chosen to be dull, or, as some of them
would claim, they have had dullness thrust upon them.

The English which fills the air that businessmen breathe
all day long, month after month, is droning, without light and
shade and entirely impersonal. Any one of a thousand people
could have written it and a highly intelligent, very able industrialist put his name to it. It is this kind of English – a good,
solid scissors and paste job which can be guaranteed neither
to hit the headlines nor to jerk an audience into instant
attention:

> The benefits of sound planning, good management, and well-
> directed investment are all being put at risk, particularly in
> the UK, by the present rate of inflation. Major corrective
> action must be the top national priority and nothing should
> be allowed to stand in its way. I do not underestimate the
> difficulties nationally of bringing about a significant reduction
> in the level of wage and salary increases, of securing an im-
> proved utilisation of labour resources, of cutting back public
> expenditure and making more effective use of that which
> remains. But all these things are essential if manufacturing
> industry is to be successful in creating the resources on which
> the growth of our national wealth totally depends.[1]

and this,

During the past few weeks we have been holding discussions with a large cross-section of well-qualified financial executives in the banking and industrial sectors. Many of them have been working in companies experiencing conditions of extreme difficulty, and have made notable contributions through their positive approach to financial planning and control, and by their ability to tackle individual problem areas affecting profitability and liquidity. We have been particularly impressed with some of the younger executives whose intellectual capabilities and personal qualities appear to mark them out for future line and financial management positions.[2]

Few people can remain entirely unaffected by a regular daily diet of this kind of glossy wordiness. Utterly unmemorable, but clearly meant to impress, it can be churned out page after page by a reasonably skilled practitioner with very little effort. It has a deadening effect on the mind and stuns and drugs, rather than communicates. It is the opium of today's business world, and those who work for long enough under its influence have their own ability to produce sharp-edged language destroyed. They can speak and write nonsense like 'the installation of excess capacity' without realising it, and they wonder why the irreverent outside world laughs when they produce gems like, 'People will discharge effluent'.

Sadly, one has to record that most management courses and business schools encourage language like the Jarratt and Blakiston specimens quoted above. Until one turns it upside down to inspect it, it looks and sounds 'professional'. It is more polished and more acceptable to say of a company, especially a large company, that it is 'experiencing conditions of extreme difficulty' than that it has almost exhausted its credit with the bank and that the public will no longer buy what it makes. And phrases like 'major corrective action must be the top national priority' sound more statesmanlike in the Chairman's mouth than 'I'm sick and tired of this Government sitting on its bottom and doing nothing. It's got to take some drastic action, and quickly.' But nobody, inside or outside the media, takes the slightest notice of the Chairman who says that 'major corrective action must be the top national priority'. They have heard such language hundreds of times before and it has lost all its power of catching the attention. It is worn out and not worth using. But the Chairman with the courage to break free from dead words and to tell his company and the world that 'I'm sick and tired of this Government sitting on its bottom and doing nothing' would be given big headlines by a grateful Press.

Previous generations of businessmen listened Sunday after Sunday to the Authorised Version of the Bible, and to the Prayer Book, translations which were written when English was still young and fresh and before it fossilised into 'the improved utilisation of labour resources' and 'their positive approach to financial planning and control'. They were reared and educated on this vigorous language and, whatever attention they may have paid to the moral precepts they expressed, they were at least aware of it as a standard. Once a week at least they were in contact with English at its best.

With the fading away of church-going and Bible-reading, the last link with rich, poetic language has gone, and all that is left is the bogus tinsel-poetry and fairground art of the Masonic ritual, the Authorised Version and Christian ritual gone bad. Automatic, computerised language has taken over and it has become extremely difficult to express one's feelings in any but the most banal and stereotyped fashion. With the emotions, as with opinions, one plays safe in public, and the result, inevitably, is that one makes no impact at all.

The psychologists have been probing, plotting and predicting human feelings and responses for more than half a century and their work has been taken up with enthusiasm by those whose main interest in life is selling. Not surprisingly, it has been discovered that fear, greed, envy and a wish to conform are powerful influences on behaviour and habit, and these are played on over and over again in advertisements and selling campaigns. The fact that they are the baser motives is of no consequence. They sell goods, whereas kindness, sympathy, prudence, resourcefulness and stoicism sell nothing.

Sex is reduced to bosoms and bottoms, and anything that money cannot buy simply does not exist. Feelings, like everything else, can be bought and sold, provided the price is right. Truth has long since been jettisoned.

Some businesses – cigarettes, pet foods, patent medicines, alcohol, cars – live entirely in this debased, corrupting atmosphere. Others – plants and seeds, timber, metals, fuel – are, as yet, comparatively free from it. But selling, like war and gambling, is an exciting activity for those who enjoy this kind of thing and any hint from outside that the selling enthusiast is making himself ridiculous by his tactics is likely to be met with blank amazement. The writer recalls a never-to-be-forgotten day spent a few years ago with the regional manager of a certain highly successful soft-drink firm. To confuse the issue, we will say that it was either Coca-Cola or Pepsi-Cola. On entering the manager's room, he was whisked – ushered would be much too sedate a term – into a chair facing the manager and became aware of a row of six opened bottles of the Product down the centre of the table. One was pushed towards the guest, almost before he had time to sit down, and another was swept up to the manager's mouth, to be gulped just as it was, straight from the bottle – the brew was too wonderful to tolerate the delay caused by drinking it through a straw or pouring it into a glass. It so happened that this particular visitor detested the Product and never drank it under any circumstances. The manager found this quite impossible to believe – he was on his second bottle of the day by this time – and launched into a selling campaign immediately, of a forcefulness designed to break down the resistance of the most stubborn heretic. When this failed, he decided the situation had become impossible to handle – it was, he made clear, quite outside his experience – and embarked on a tour of the plant, pointing out the extreme attention to cleanliness, the happy, enthusiastic faces of the workers and the impossibility of any customer receiving even a single bottle which deviated a fraction from the internationally laid down standard. To ensure this, every scrap of mineral content, life and individuality was scientifically removed from the local water used in the manufacturing process, so that one started with a completely neutral base.

After an hour of this, we left for a drive round the outskirts of London to visit another of the company's factories. Throughout the journey, the Regional Manager, who was driving, played tape-recordings of what he called 'selling-situations', real-life occasions on which various of his salesmen were attempting to sell the Product, sometimes successfully, sometimes not. As the cassettes wound on, he produced a steady flow of comments on tactics and techniques, completely involving himself in what was going on. Time, he explained, was far too precious to be spent in mere driving and he had trained himself to do these two things at once, just as his salesmen were trained to record themselves at work and to deliver the tapes to him in batches for vetting.

An outsider could only marvel. This was a creature from another planet, working to rules and standards one knew nothing about. To the man immediately concerned, however, they represented the norm and there was nothing in the least crazy or ridiculous about them. The row of bottles, replenished throughout the day; the worship of the Product; the murderous pressure and the frequent excitement; the tape-playing; the extraordinary house-language; the view of life as one enormous never-ending selling campaign, to which one was wholly devoted – all this represented life, the real world. To stand aside from it and look at it objectively with a layman's eye was as unthinkable as an outside view of Christianity would have been to a medieval Christian. To be of the Faith was to believe totally and to be totally involved.

It is not easy to persuade people who live their lives in this way that, when they emerge from their working-world to give a talk or an interview, the general public may well find their language and their attitudes puzzling and funny. Phrases like 'the image of gas in the Seventies', 'soft-furnishing consumer-satisfaction', 'a low-keel bird' and 'cost per volume of drink' may be normal to the person who uses them, but his listeners are liable to find them merely bewildering and absurd. The response will consequently be quite different from what was intended.

Somehow, in order to put one's company, job, profession or organisation across, one simply must try to see it as the outside world sees it, warts, misdeeds, blunders and all. The man who cannot do this is inadequate as a company spokesman and unconvincing as a human being, but to achieve it demands a determined effort to mix with a wide range of people and to listen to their conversation, often as an eavesdropper. Paradoxically, it is more difficult to do this nowadays than it was fifty or a hundred years ago. The custom today is to live one's life in a more or less hermetically sealed layer, and the biggest single cause of this is the motor-car. If one travels regularly by bus or train, it is almost impossible not to overhear at least bits and pieces of the conversation of a cross-section of one's fellow citizens, although for those who travel first-class the cross-section is not so satisfactory. By closing one's eyes and pretending to be asleep, the most astonishing range of information and opinion can come one's way during the course of a railway journey. One can also do quite well in crowded pubs, at bus-stations and at bus-stops and in large stores.

However, the higher an executive climbs, the less likely he is to travel by train or Tube, to visit crowded pubs or to spend much time in the kind of places where the bulk of the nation does its shopping. He will move about in the little closed world of his car or of taxis, he will eat and drink with people on his own level, who share his prejudices and habits and, although he may persuade himself that he keeps in touch with what the man in the street thinks, he almost certainly deludes himself as much as Trade Union leaders do, who are always convinced that, because their heart is in the right place and they have the proper origins, they are bound to know what they are pleased to call working people feel about every possible issue – and often make serious mistakes, simply because they are isolated from the people they lead. The old-style employer, who walked round his works or office every day and chatted to the men, who used public transport and who had a succession of gardeners, cooks, maids and char-women in and out of his house was much more successfully tuned in to the idiom and pattern of thinking of ordinary people than the majority of present-day employed executives.

There are, of course, certain substitutes for personal con-tact, but, although they are better than nothing, they are not the equal of the real thing. One can, for instance, listen to people being interviewed on television and radio. Radio, on the whole, offers the better opportunities, mainly in its local and national magazine programmes, which draw in a large selection of people of all types during a week. It is important to bear in mind, however, that broadcasting is mainly on the lookout for what might be called extraordinary ordinary people and that such people will be mentally spruced up for the occasion, with their pattern of talking disciplined either by the interviewer, whose business it is to control the shape and length of the item, or by the editor of the tape or film, who will simply remove the hesitations, the repetition and the long windedness, a kindly service, which is, of course, available to everyone who broadcasts, business executives included.

A really good public relations department – and there are not, alas, many of them – functions as a two-way filter between the company and the public. It passes outwards, usually to the press and to the broadcasting organisations, what it thinks the public ought to know about the company's current activities and problems, answers enquiries and collects and digests the feelings of the outside world about the company and its products. The in-coming function is the one that is usually neglected and yet it is of great importance and can be extremely helpful to those members of an organisation who have to do a good deal of speaking to outside bodies. Many concerns, probably the majority, have no idea of what the district or the country thinks about them, and, so long as they can sell what they make and get the staff they need, they can see no reason to find out. The result is that their executives, who are saturated with the results of market research about customers and products, but who are usually fed with extremely meagre information about the company itself, are forced to go into battle one-armed and half-blind. They are expected to keep on shouting from the housetops, 'we belong to a great organisation', only to discover, to their horror and discomfiture, that the public does not think that at all.

In the recent past – the situation has improved somewhat recently as the result of a harsher economic climate – many highly placed men have been, to put the matter bluntly, cocooned. They have been told what they would get pleasure from hearing and unwelcome nastinesses have been kept from them. Men coddled in this way have been liable to find television interviewers 'rude', 'aggressive', 'left-wing' and even 'unpatriotic', when all that was in fact happening to them was that they were being asked pointed questions of a kind that normally never came their way and for which they had no training or experience. One could put this another way, by saying that a large number of important people, in Britain and elsewhere, have been used to living in a club-atmosphere, in which remarks are not made which might disturb the peace and tone of the club. Most public appearances, however, are likely to take place on occasions where the club rules do not apply, and where a speaker has to show considerable agility and quick-wittedness in adapting himself to a completely different set of assumptions. Some businessmen find this exceedingly difficult, and their performance shows it.

Two examples, one from the shoe industry and one from brewing, may make the point clearer. The brewers as a whole were not well pleased by the article which appeared in a Sunday newspaper on the subject of the strength of different brands of beer on the market. There were tables comparing the various beers in each price-range, and it was obvious – and gently pointed out by the writer of the article – that one particular manufacturer was consistently at the bottom of each league table. Predictably, the company's public relations officer was called from his bed, or the garden, or wherever he happened to be at the time and told to do something about it forthwith. Like a sensible man, he brooded over the matter for an hour or so and then telephoned the managing director to ask for a statement which he would make sure was prominently featured in the licensed trade's newspaper the following morning, which was, of course, a Monday. The statement duly appeared and it was to the effect that one had to be very careful about using phrases like 'the strength of beer' and 'specific gravity', because these things were not necessarily what they seemed and, anyway, there was far more to beer than mere strength. Colour, taste, smoothness, all these were of vital importance, as any publican or beer-drinking man or woman would tell you.

By this time, the television newsrooms were beginning to read their morning papers and were sensing comic possibilities in the story. There was plenty of time to work it up during the day, and by the time the evening bulletins and news magazines went out, three lines of attack had emerged, all of which were put to representatives of the brewers, the licensees and, of course, the general public. First, if the figures meant nothing and to talk about 'the strength of beer' was a nonsense, why was it, even so, that some firms did so much better in the tables than others? Second, was beer, as the article suggested, getting steadily weaker and weaker as the years went by? And, thirdly, weren't some brewers charging an awful lot of money for something little better than coloured water?

All this was, of course, outside-the-club nonsense and people who could ever think of questions like these were totally unfit for decent company. Beer was the Englishman's drink and there was no more honest and patriotic a body of men in the country than the brewers. And, anyway, would a company have survived and prospered for more than a century if it hadn't given the customers what they wanted?

At this point, a God-given working man was brought into a northern studio to say that what the beer was like, strong or weak, wasn't of the least significance. It was the place you drank it in and the people you were with that mattered. What was more, he thundered, and he was glad to have the chance of saying it with millions listening, these modern, swanky, drawing-room pubs the brewers were building were enough to make any beer taste awful.

This was the genuine voice of the man on the Salford omnibus, the voice that somehow fails to penetrate the brewery boardrooms and gets missed out in the market research reports. It may or may not be relevant to mention that the company concerned was bought out not long after the incident recorded and absorbed into a bigger group. High-powered executives certainly go round with their ears and eyes closed at their peril and a little systematic slumming does no harm at all.

The footwear story illustrates a similar Mandarin quality and lack of sensitivity. The occasion was what was described as a Consumer Brains Trust, and it took place in a large provincial city. One member of the three man and one woman panel was a director of a large firm of shoe manufacturers, and a question put by a woman sitting close to the front of this quite large audience was clearly aimed mainly at him. Why, she wanted to know, was it impossible for her to buy a pair of his company's shoes, to wear herself, which would keep out the water? 'Madam,' he replied from his platform height, 'if you want something that's guaranteed to keep your feet dry, you should buy yourself a pair of rubber boots.'

This was not, as it happened, a particularly clever remark to make, and both the audience and his fellow panel members turned on the speaker and slaughtered him. A moment's reflexion and a little more sensitivity and a little less arrogance would have led to a more successful approach. It is not a good thing to suggest to a lady, of whatever age, that she should go about in rubber boots if she wishes to keep her feet dry. In Britain, it rains frequently and to be condemned to spend much of her time shod like this is not a prospect that many women are likely to relish. There is, in fact, nothing unreasonable at all in expecting to buy ordinary walking shoes that will keep the weather out. With high fashion shoes it is, admittedly, more of a problem, but the tactless director had no cause to think that the question was concerned with high fashion shoes. On several counts, he earns no marks at all. To begin with, he was there as the representative of a local firm, and the impression he made on his audience certainly did the reputation of his firm no good at all. Then, anyone as grossly provoked as this woman undoubtedly was, is very likely to say, publicly, 'Very well. If your firm's shoes won't keep my feet dry, I shall find somebody else's that will', which is exactly what she did say, to the applause of the audience. That reaction must have cancelled out the value of several thousand pounds' worth of advertising expenditure, since if one thing is certain in business it is that one dissatisfied customer will tell her friends and acquaintances about the manufacturer's failure to please her and that one person can become a hundred in no time at all.

Looking at the speaker and listening to his decidedly I-know-best-and-who-are-you-to-question-it manner, and knowing something of his career and background, one had good reason to believe that he would not have dealt with a similar question coming from a man in quite the same way. There was something in his attitude and tone of voice that suggested 'Silly little woman'. He felt, all too obviously, that he was addressing a member of an inferior breed.

Many businessmen, regrettably, contrive to give the same impression. For reasons which we will discuss in a moment, they find it impossible to treat women as equals, and make many enemies in a mixed audience as a result. In particular, they often find it difficult to understand that a television audience, for the kind of programme on which they are most likely to appear, contains at least 50 per cent women, most of whom will be regarding him as a person, pleasant or unpleasant, rather than as an oracle.

It is the average businessman's misfortune, not shared by those who work in the Civil Service, education, broadcasting, journalism or publishing, that in the course of his work he meets very few intelligent women on anything like equal terms, and not a great many socially either. His contacts,

arguments, idea-swapping and eating and drinking are over-
whelmingly with men. In the world in which he moves,
women are essentially subordinate creatures, who exist to
carry out orders and to please him. The result of such a situation, continued over many years, is to fail to realise that few
women have a businessman's values. Many women enjoy
positions of responsibility, but it is only extremely rarely that
they are willing to sacrifice themselves on the altar of ambition
and to make their job their whole life. They are, on the whole,
more honest and less open to corruption than men, both in
business and in public life, although it has been pointed out
often enough that women are exposed to fewer financial
temptations than men. There are those who believe, with
some evidence to support their theory, that, given the opportunity, women are quite as likely as men to indulge in forgery
and embezzlement, which are crimes of greed. Bribery, however, seems to be, as yet, a male, rather than a female habit.
It is worth noting, in this connexion, that of the public servants, local government officials and business people mentioned
and prosecuted in connexion with the bribery scandal which
shook Britain during 1973–74 and which involved contracts
given to Poulsons, one of the country's biggest architectural
firms, all were men. Women are much less likely to be prepared to take short cuts in either business or the professions.
They prefer to go for jobs which are worth doing in human
terms and, with rare exceptions, the pursuit of power or
money for its own sake does not interest them. They do not,
of course, belong to their male colleagues' clubs or secret
societies and, in private, they find both somewhat ludicrous,
uncivilised and non-adult, which indeed they are.

The first step, both for men and women, is to recognise this
situation, and the second is to come to terms with it, by becoming aware that the best speakers display a subtle mixture
of both male and female characteristics, a statement which
will not be popular in certain quarters. The 100 per cent males
and 100 per cent females, or at least the people who choose to
present this kind of front to the world, are boring to listen to

and make little impact on the minds of their audience, whatever they may do to their bodies, and to certain of their emotions.

An inexperienced or unsuccessful speaker is frequently told, 'Relax and be yourself' which is, for most people, a fairly useless piece of advice, if one is appearing as a spokesman for one's employers. The fear of departing from the party line robs many speakers of confidence. They are anxious to make a good job of what they are doing, eager to sound at ease and in control of the situation, anxious to please their listeners, but nagging away all the time at them is the fear of what their wife, children, boss, colleagues and friends are going to say to them afterwards, or, even worse, what they are going to think without saying. There are certain remedies which can be taken against this complaint and they will be described later, but meanwhile it may be of some comfort to mention that whatever one may think one's viewing and listening friends and enemies are getting ready to say afterwards it will nearly always be something completely different from what one has in mind or dreads. It will not be, 'why did you say 30,000, when it was 20,000?', or 'you hinted that our drivers are thieves. We shall have a strike on our hands tomorrow', but 'Your tie wasn't straight', or 'you looked as if you hadn't been to sleep for a week', or 'why did you keep twitching your mouth like that?' However carefully they may have been prepared, and however brilliantly they may be presented, one's golden words and thoughts are more than likely to make a much less lasting impression than one's appearance and mannerisms, which is both a humbling and a reassuring thought.

NOTES AND REFERENCES

1. Alex Jarratt, of Reed International, quoted in *The Times*, July 1, 1975.
2. Advertisement by Michael Blakiston and Co., in *The Times*, May 24, 1975.

4. Getting to grips with the fundamental problems

It will be seen, from Chapters Two and Three, that the faults which make for a poor public performance fall into two groups. We might call them the Ignorance Group and the Fear Group. In this chapter we shall indicate ways of dealing with both of these, and of building an effective personal style, which emphasises one's strong points and plays down and conceals the weak ones.

It is absolutely essential to begin with oneself and work outwards, not to look around for models and then try to adapt to them. This means a methodical, ruthless, but friendly look at what one looks like and how one sounds. The ideal way of doing this is with the help of a video-tape recorder, but a sound tape-recorder and a mirror are better than nothing. Photographs are practically useless, partly because they are posed and partly because they cannot show the body in movement and one expression of the face shading off into another. Every organisation of any size should provide simple video-tape facilities for its employees, which can be used at any time for an appearance and voice check. Having viewed and listened to themselves critically, with the kind of analytical tools which the present book aims to provide, most intelligent people can begin to map out a road towards improvement for themselves.

It should be mentioned that black and white television, which is what is usually available on closed-circuit, makes the majority of men and women look ten years younger than they really are, assuming, of course, that the lighting is competently arranged. For some of us this is a decided advantage, but those who have reached positions of responsibility at a youthful age may well yearn for a more mature appearance than they see on the screen in front of them.

Whether one sees oneself in black and white or in full colour, however, a little courage and practice will soon allow one to say, 'This, stripped of all vanity and pretence, is what I really look like. This is the person an audience has presented to them.' The shock soon passes, and, in most cases, it is possible to take an objective interest in the man in front of one's eyes. These are his large, bushy eyebrows, these are his sticking-out ears, this is his mouth, which smiles much less than its owner suspected, and which is always a little down on the left-hand side. This is the man who is trying so hard to look dignified and is finishing up merely by looking gloomy, secretive and depressing. This is the executive who looks much too pros-perous and slick for safety, and who had better take steps to democratise himself a little. This, in sum and in detail, is the raw material with which one starts, the foundations on which one builds, and it is useful to make notes of how it all appears.

A typical piece of visual self-assessment might read like this:

> I have a long, rather fleshy face, with more of a double chin than pleases me. I think I shave carefully, but my jaws are distinctly blue. My eyes look rather hard and unsympathetic and I don't seem to change my expression very much as I talk. The dark lines under my eyes make me look distinctly sinister. I don't appear to enjoy life a great deal and, for some reason I don't quite understand, I seem to be on the defensive. Not a very friendly, welcoming kind of face at all.

These comments on one's appearance should be matched with an attempt to describe one's voice and accent, together with any mannerisms of which one is conscious. This can profitably be done in two stages, one before analysing a record-ing and one afterwards. The two impressions can be very different, the first being based on years of wishful thinking, masochism, self-deception and on remarks, both flattering and the reverse, from one's family and colleagues, and the second on what one hopes will be a good deal closer to reality.

Here are some pre-recording notes made by a selection of senior executives from a variety of organisations, and set out on a form under prescribed headings.

a. *What impression do I probably make on people?*
b. *How would I describe my voice and accent?*
c. *Which of my mannerisms are particularly noticeable?*

Marketing Manager (45)

a. 'Probably varies between those who think me too glib and those who think me naïve. The most flattering would say articulate and sincere.'
b. 'Thin, occasionally faltering, north-country origin of my parents shows through some public school overlay. When excited, my volume goes up too much.'
c. 'My wife criticises my scratching habits.'

Director of Research, Plastics Company (48)

a. 'Possibly rather reserved, not forthcoming, intellectual. I say this, not because it is what I think I am, but what I have been told. I hope I take sufficient trouble to overcome this in front of an audience, but it may still come out with strangers in casual conversation.'
b. 'Southern. Gravelly.'
c. 'Tendency to pepper my sentences with "you know", when I am embarrassed or when I am pursuing an argument in which I do not have full confidence.'

Financial Controller (53)

a. 'Straightforward and outspoken, but open to reasoned argument – at least I like to think so.'
b. 'Fruity, with a Yorkshire accent.'
c. 'A tendency to repeat "you know".'

Regional Officer, United Nations Association (Woman, 60)

a. 'I am possibly considered a bit standoffish and hard to get through to. I am sure this is produced by an inborn shyness. I have tried all my life to overcome this. The fact is, I love human nature.'
b. 'Voice soft. No pronounced accent.'
c. 'Nervous movement of hands and fingers.'

Corporate Development Manager, Rubber Company (43)

a. 'Remote and detached, but enthusiastic when the subject interests me.'
b. 'Public school. Cambridge. Lack of fluency.'
c. 'Too frequent changes of facial expression.'

General Manager, Tobacco Company (41)

a. 'I have been told that I have a degree of directness that does not always please others. Equally, I am not well known for being tolerant.'
b. 'Deep voice. Neutral accent.'
c. 'I tend to pull the lobe of my right ear when I am bored.'

Technical Sales Manager (31)

a. 'Reasonably polite, but inclined to be outspoken.'
b. 'Too high-pitched. My voice is a London–Somerset hybrid of the worst type.'
c. 'Gesticulatory movements.'

It is of no particular consequence whether these personal assessments are accurate or not. Their value is that they are an essential first step towards something which a surprisingly large number of people seem to lack, an interest in themselves as they really are. They may say that they have a strong Midland accent, when a trained observer fails to detect more than a trace, or they may describe their manner as 'blunt', when what they really mean is, 'Holding the position I do, I want to sound blunt. This is how I ought to sound.' On the other hand, people who have been accustomed to think of themselves as genial and forthcoming may be staggered to hear that they sound rude, abrupt and aggressive on the telephone.

The number of people who believe they are not sufficiently fluent or that they say 'er' too much suggests something that is certainly true, that a high proportion of businessmen believe that the ideal speaker, the kind of speaker they themselves would like to be, is the person who never stops and never has to pause to think or to draw breath. Over and over again, one has to point out that the greatest skill in speaking to any kind or size of audience is not talking, but pausing, and that the surest sign of a speaker who is lacking in confidence and experience is that he has not mastered the art of pausing.

The root of the trouble is a failure to distinguish between the kind of pause which occurs when one has lost a train of thought or is unable to find the right word and the kind which comes from a speaker who is completely in control of the situation. To anyone whose main fear is of drying up, the never-stop, dripping-tap style will be a matter of envy and longing, but, for most people, the attempt to get from beginning to end of a sentence, a paragraph or, most absurd of all, a complete talk, without a break is kind neither to oneself nor to one's audience. What needs to be cultivated and studied is the technique of the strategic pause.

The time and place for a pause is before and after one makes an important point. The first pause should be preceded by a phrase or sentence to wake one's listeners up and prepare them for what is about to come and the second pause can often be followed to great effect by a consolidating phrase, which pushes the point home once again. This illustrates the method:

> And I remember once when I was much younger than I am now, mixing my drinks in an absolutely disastrous fashion. *TWO SECOND PAUSE.* I had two large vodkas and then, very stupidly, followed them with a cup of tea. *ONE SECOND*

PAUSE. I passed right out and stayed unconscious for nearly five hours. *TWO SECOND PAUSE*. I learnt my lesson the hard way. Never, ever, drink anything after vodka, not even a cup of tea.

The first pause here creates the necessary suspense and anticipation, the second keeps the audience on tenterhooks and the third ties in the ends of the story. Without these pauses, half the impact of the story disappears. As actors in search of a laugh know very well, the timing is everything and experience is very largely experience of getting the timing right.

As we have indicated previously, there is no more reason to despair of one's accent than of one's face. Certain accents, however, like certain faces, are better suited to one kind of occasion than to another. In today's world, the most fortunate person is the one who has a basically neutral accent, not suggesting any particular region or social background, but who has a sufficiently flexible mind and a sufficiently well-tuned ear to be able to adjust what we might term the cruising accent slightly upwards or downwards to match the company of the moment. This is a particularly valuable talent for those whose work depends on getting quickly on easy terms with a wide range of people. It should be emphasised with all possible force, however, that this does not mean deliberately adopting a bogus, uneducated form of speech, simply because one is talking to an uneducated person. Speech-slumming is as insulting, patronising and absurd as any other kind of slumming. All that is being suggested is that it is an advantage to modify one's social accent fractionally in order to move slightly closer towards the other person, and the direction of that movement may be either upwards or downwards.

Most people can improve their sensitivity with practice. Now and again, it is worth making a conscious effort to listen to another person's voice with exceptional care and to try to answer these questions about it.

a. Can I guess where he spent his boyhood and his teens?

b. Can I detect more than one area in his accent?
c. Does he sound as if he has made a deliberate effort to 'improve' his accent? What do I think of the result?
d. If I knew nothing about him at all, and if I were meeting him for the first time, where would I place him socially?
e. How does his accent and his voice affect me personally? If I like it, why do I like it? If I dislike it, why do I dislike it?

One can play this game as easily with the people one meets artificially on television as with those who come one's way in face-to-face situations. To be able to play it accurately and well is an important management tool, but it is helpful to remember that it is a game in which everyone is a performer and everyone, at least potentially, an analyst. If I am listening to him like this, I must reckon that he is doing the same to me. It can become an absorbing game and, by bringing a seldom discussed and, indeed, often taboo subject out into the open, a number of fears and uncertainties can be removed.

'Am I being pompous?' and 'Do I really feel what I'm saying I feel?' are also helpful exercises. If these questions are found too difficult to begin with, one can always develop the habit by listening to other people first and then transferring the technique to an examination of oneself. If the answer to the first question is 'Yes' and to the second 'No', one is able to say, 'What does this really amount to?' and the translation has a very different flavour from the original.

Suppose, for instance, we had decided to examine the speeches made for and against continuing British member-ship of the Common Market during the referendum cam-paign of 1975. How frequently did we feel inclined to say, 'That man's just pouring out grand-sounding words that add up to nothing', or 'That woman doesn't really believe that old age pensioners are going to be half-starved if we stay in the EEC. She's just a professional politician playing on the heart-strings.'? The first person was guilty of pomposity – phrases full of nothing but air – and the second of sentiment-ality – pretending to have emotions she didn't in fact have.

What is really being advocated in a series of self-imposed translation exercises in order to improve one's ability to distinguish between the bogus and the genuine and in this way to get into better speaking and writing training oneself, by sweating and dieting off the mental fat and flabbiness that prevent one from getting to grips with an audience. Exercises of this kind can be a great help in lessening the widespread fear of straightforward language which is at the root of most communication problems. Once the words of this distinguished industrialist or that minister are proved not to pass any information into one's own mind, the warning should be plain: 'Get your thoughts clear and put them across as simply and directly as you can, or you're going to talk as much useless rubbish as that man'. Do, in fact, as you would be done by.

Here is an example of misleading oratory, from a man of some eminence in British public life, Mr Hugh Jenkins, the Minister Responsible for the Arts. The holder of this post might be expected to be interested above the average in clarity of thought and precision of language, but an incident at the 1975 Annual Conference of the Museums Association suggested that Mr Jenkins was a professional politician first and Minister for the Arts second. In his address to the Conference he criticised the composition of the important, if not all-important, link between the museum profession and the Government, the Standing Commission on Museums and Galleries. 'I am horrified.' he said, 'at the extraordinary element of aristocracy to be found in the Standing Commission. One would imagine that only those with titles were interested in art.'[1] Now Mr Jenkins was not really horrified at all. The composition of the Standing Commission did not cause his hair to stand on end, his face to turn deathly pale and his limbs to tremble. He intended his equation of 'aristocracy' and 'titles' to confuse the issue – for every member of the aristocracy in Britain there are at least fifty with titles, many of them members and supporters of Mr Jenkins' own party. Are such Labour Party stalwarts as Lord George-Brown, Lady Falkender or Lord Greene (formerly Mr Sid Greene

of the NUR), to be considered members of the aristocracy?
Or Lord Feather, Lord Collison or Lord Cooper, all of them
life peers of impeccable trade union lineage? Or the dozens of
Labour knights? Would Mr Jenkins be horrified at their
inclusion on the Museums Commission? Or could it be, perhaps, that his remarks were only aimed at those titled people
who are known to be friends of the Conservative party and
that Conservatives with titles are reckoned to be automatically aristocratic and Labour people with titles something
quite different? Did he mean that anybody with any sort of
title at all should be barred, *ipso facto*, from the Standing
Commission?

There is, in any case, a fairly considerable difference
between being 'interested in art' and being sufficiently knowl-
edgeable and experienced in such matters to be fitted to give
the kind of judgment and advice that falls to the lot of the
Commission, which has, among other tasks, the immensely
difficult and unenviable responsibility of deciding to which
museums and art galleries those treasures which come to the
nation in lieu of death duties shall go. This is hardly to be
done properly by people whose only qualification is that they
are 'interested in the arts'. What, in any case, does 'interested
in the arts' mean? Which arts? Would suitable recruits be
men and women who go to the theatre or the cinema from
time to time, or who paint or sculpt as a hobby or who enjoy
photography?

What Mr Jenkins was, in fact, saying was something like
this: 'There are several Conservatives with titles on the
Standing Commission and it would do me a lot of political
good if I were to engineer their removal and their replacement
by known Labour supporters, one or two of whom could
quite conveniently be "democrats", i.e. long-service Labour
councillors from the Museums and Libraries Committees in
solid, industrial places like Bradford and Stoke-on-Trent.'
A plain statement like this, however, might well have inter-
fered with Mr Jenkins' political future, and it was therefore
wrapped up in the language we have just dissected.

Partly as a means of self-defence and partly as a means of improving our own use of English, we should all make a habit of turning passages like this inside out fairly frequently. The exercise can be exceedingly stimulating and a way second to none of sorting out the men in public life who are worth something and those who are worth nothing at all. If some of one's own colleagues suffer in the process, so much the better for our long-suffering society.

There is an ample supply, in any country, of well-known public figures who can always be relied on to provide first-class material for translation practice. The European Commissioner for External Relations and our former Ambassador in Paris, Sir Christopher Soames, for instance, is frequently worth attention. Speaking at a meeting of the European Conservative Forum in Brussels during the summer of 1975, he said:

> When we ask ourselves the question, 'What sort of Europe?' – issues of economic and monetary policy, of social policy, of external relations – we could find it difficult to discover common ground to reach concrete and practical conclusions in every sphere.
>
> So a balance must be found which combines the greatest possible advantage in respect of consumer choice and economic logic, with the least disadvantage in respect of standardisation and centralised regulation.
>
> I believe that, in the concept of 'optional' harmonisation which has now largely replaced the earlier emphasis on a universal regulation, we have found the right balance which can have the support of all the elements of the centre-right.
>
> The 'optional' approach enables you to produce whatever is required for consumption on the home market, while the obstacles to international trade inside the Community in the item in question are removed so long as certain common standards are met.[2]

It is possible that Sir Christopher, like other well-known and ambitious men, was interested on this occasion not so much in the audience immediately in front of him as in those who

would read the reports of his speech in the world's newspapers
and periodicals. He could rely on his name and position to
bring applause from his audience, whether they understood
what he was saying or not. In any case, the flavour of his.
language was obviously right, even if his flow of words was
not such as to foster perfect understanding between himself
and his listeners. It is not spoken English at all, but, when
one has the text to read, re-read and ponder over, it is possible
to make some sort of sense of it.

What it amounts to, in plain terms is this.

> Economically, socially, politically, Europe is a disorderly
> mess, and it's very difficult to find standardised ways of making
> and selling things which are going to work in every country
> of the EEC. Compulsory regulations won't work, but, by
> using a little common sense and persuasion, we ought to be
> able, in each of our countries, to produce what our own people
> want and that's of the right design and quality to find a market
> abroad as well. And I reckon this is the kind of approach that
> all European Conservatives can agree to.

These are words one can speak and which an audience can
understand. Why, then, did Sir Christopher, who is an
intelligent and cultured man, produce such vague pomposi-
ties? The answer is that both speaker and audience were
wrapped in the chains of a thoroughly bad tradition which
make it difficult to use simple, straightforward language and
to maintain face. The tradition is getting weaker in patches,
but it is still exceedingly strong in politics and in international
organisations, where it is thought to be highly dangerous to
use language which means something definite and concrete.
Sir Christopher was expressing himself in thoroughly statesmanlike language, but if, when he had sat down, the members
of his audience had each been given a piece of paper and
asked to write down a very brief summary of what he had
said, the results would have made interesting reading. The
test is a fair one, but few speakers ever receive the benefits
of it. 'What,' one should make a point of asking oneself on

every possible occasion, 'has that man just said?' If little or nothing remains in one's memory, the speaker, however eminent, can safely be written off as incompetent.

One may, of course, proceed the other way round, with great profit, by deciding before speaking, exactly what the core of one's address is intended to be, and then writing it down in no more than three or four sentences. One's task then becomes much clearer. It can be divided into three parts:

1. To please the audience, to make oneself liked.
2. To keep it awake and interested, so that it is in a fit state to receive the message.
3. To make sure that, whatever else passes it by, it goes away having understood and absorbed beyond any doubt what we have called the core-information.

The summary can read like this:

> We've had a lot of trouble with these rubber dinghies of ours ever since we first put them on the market three years ago. The material and the construction just haven't been strong enough and customers have always been complaining about the boats leaking. But at last, thank God, we've cured the problem and we're sure that what we're selling now's a really reliable article.

or this:

> It doesn't give us any pleasure at all when our gas mains blow up, and we're desperately sorry when there are accidents and people get killed and injured and buildings destroyed. The real trouble is that the kind of soil we've got round here plays hell with the iron pipes, and the ones that have been down 50 years or more have got very thin and dangerous in some areas. But the new pipes we're laying now stand up to the conditions and once we've replaced all the old ones there shouldn't be any further bother. It's bound to take several years to do it, though.

or this:

> We've got to close this works down, after making clay tiles here for more than a hundred years. We hate to do it, and it

isn't because we're inefficient or badly organised. The reason is that we can't meet the competition from concrete and asbestos-cement roofing tiles. They don't look as pleasant and they won't last as long, but they're cheaper and, under present conditions, that's all that builders and architects think about.

If hard thinking fails to produce a summary of this type, the likelihood is that one is faced with a non-occasion, with nothing really to say. It is possible to carry off such an occasion with a certain amount of credit, but it demands skill and luck, and one should recognise the difficult ground on which one stands.

If one accepts that something very close to a conversational manner is normally much more likely to be successful and that anything grander or more formal is much more likely to get the speaker into practical difficulties, there are certain techniques worth considering, in order to make such a style easier to achieve.

Whenever possible, at least until the style is fully formed, one should do one's best to sit, rather than stand, to speak. The temptation to orate is much easier to resist sitting down. It is not, of course, necessary to sit on a chair. Most audiences take very well to a man sitting, or half-sitting, on the corner of a table, although for a woman it is sometimes a little more difficult, and a position like this leaves one pleasantly free to use one's arms and hands to the full in support of the points one is making. Sitting on a table is not very different from sitting on a stool at a bar and if one can keep the bar associations well in mind when talking, an easy, relaxed manner is difficult to avoid. The chair-at-a-table position is better for the inexperienced speaker than standing at a lectern, which invites the lecturing manner and the heavy use of notes, but it is not such a simple matter to maintain close contact with the audience in this way, unless it is a very small one, of almost committee size.

Always use a microphone in a large hall, and complain if one is not provided. The halter-type microphone, which is

small and light and slung round the neck is far preferable to
the stand type. It allows the speaker to sit or stand where he
pleases and to move about without causing difficulties for the
technicians. But any microphone makes it possible to work at
a conversational, person-to-person level, which is what one
wants, and to avoid the dreadfully artificial, formal Oxford
Union style, which was developed in pre-microphone days
and has been the curse of British platform speaking ever since.

Speaking from a prepared script needs a great deal of
practice and acting ability and very few people do it well. As
we have said earlier, the job is made much easier by writing
the script in one's own spoken style, but, even so, one has to
pay very careful attention to maintaining a speaking, rather
than a reading, rhythm and intonation, and to spending the
minimum amount of time looking down at the words on the
script. The right place for a speaker's eyes is looking at selected members of his audience, not at a script, and the only way
in which to do this is to train oneself to pick large blocks of
words off the paper each time one casts a glance at it. One
should, by the way, never attempt to look at or speak to an
audience as a whole. The best method is to settle from the
beginning on no more than half a dozen people, well scattered
over the room, and to rotate one's attention around these six.
This allows a direct, personal approach, with everyone else
in the vicinity imagining that the speaker is aiming his
remarks at them.

So far, we have been talking mainly of weaknesses born of
fear and we have suggested various ways of overcoming
those fears and difficulties. The weaknesses arising from
ignorance, from not having enough in one's head, are a much
more serious matter and it does nobody any good to gloss
over them or to hint, very dishonestly, that everything is
really a matter of technique. However, some forms of
ignorance are more disastrous than others and some only
become apparent when one ventures outside one's own specialist field or working atmosphere.

The general public is likely to assume that men and women

who hold positions of power and authority have considerable knowledge of the world and its affairs. This is probably flattering. Few of us reach the age of forty without realising how ignorant we are of so many things and this kind of self-awareness, which should ideally lead to an attractive humility, is not necessarily a disadvantage, providing it does not result in an inferiority complex and in a wish to draw a screen around oneself. We can, however, pick out three types of ignorance which are certainly serious and which one must somehow do something about if one wants to communicate one's ideas and personality to a wide public.

They are, not in any particular order of importance:

1. An inadequate feeling for the language and an inability to use its full resources.
2. A lack of interest in other people's lives, talents, limitations, values and responses.
3. A poor sense of history and of one's own place in it.

All three can contribute to fragile confidence, to difficulty in handling hostile or unforeseen questions and to an inadequate, or sometimes non-existent awareness of the communication problems between oneself and one's audience. Taken together, they amount to a lack of perspective, tact, discrimination and subtlety, all of which are essential qualities for a really successful speaker to possess. They can all be remedied by reading writers who make demands on one's intelligence and concentration and who really understand how to handle their mother-tongue, and by regularly taking part in conversations of which the subject matter is something better than cars, holidays, the price of everything, and other cocktail party snobberies and inanities.

Ask a hundred high-ranking executives what books have been engaging their attention recently and it will soon be discovered that the average British or American businessman's reading is a disgrace to any civilised person. There are, of course, exceptions, but, in the experience of the present author, the great majority of these leaders of our national political and economic life confine their reading to tired-mind stuff which makes absolutely no demands on them whatever. When pressed on the point, a surprisingly large number confess to reading no books at all. They are magazine and newspaper men entirely, which is another way of saying that one part of their mind, a highly important part, is permanently out of training. A carefully planned, well-written book provides an unequalled opportunity of coming into contact with better and more disciplined minds than one's own, and, above all, with different minds, minds which feed on other things. One often hears the argument that television has made books obsolete, that the ability to read a book, as distinct from dipping into it for information, is one of yesterday's skills. This is merely convenient, lazy nonsense. A lot of people are flicked on and off the television screen in the course of a week and a few of them say interesting things, but one has no opportunity to check back on what they have said, to examine it at leisure and at one's own pace, and to digest it. A kaleidoscope – and television is no more than an elaborate and expensive kaleidoscope – is all very well in its way, and an amusing toy, but it requires no effort on the part of the observer who watches its pictures flit by. In any case, even the best of television programmes is no more than the highest common factor of several minds – a producer, an editor, a commentator or presenter, and a host of technicians. It may have a central figure, the 'subject' of the programme or the item, but he does not control the shape or size of the final product, in the way a writer does a book. He is simply the principal character.

Television can be a useful and agreeable introduction to other people's worlds and those worlds will necessarily include ideas and values. It may on occasion present disturbing material or images which remain in the mind for a long while afterwards. A television programme can provide excellent entertainment and, very occasionally, it can be a considerable work of art. It can weaken prejudices, show that improbable things can be interesting, draw back the curtain from parts of the world one is unlikely to visit oneself, and make or break the reputations of public figures. We watch it and it has become part of our daily lives. But it is no more a substitute for reading than the cinema or the theatre is. It has different limitations and different opportunities, and over a day or a week the choice it offers is very restricted, a fact which comforts millions of people and causes only a few tens of thousands – a stubborn, non-assimilated, non-conforming élite – feelings of frustration and deprivation.

If the masses can find all the entertainment they want on television and no longer need to read novels in order to amuse themselves, and, if the public for intelligent books is likely to get smaller rather than larger, both of which seem probable, the question which a businessman has to answer is: 'Am I really a superior member of the herd, a mass-man with a difference, or am I an élite-figure in disguise?' Sometimes, it is true, the herd-quality takes over completely and our businessman shows remarkably few superior characteristics, and sometimes the disguise is so good that the élitist never appears from underneath it, but, in general, the British tradition makes it difficult to carry off the rôle of an intellectual and favours the uncommon man who has the instincts and tastes of the common man. This, one might suggest, is what is wrong, not only with British and American business, but with Britain and America; big common men have been trying to lead little common men for far too long, and it is high time the job was taken over by some uncommon men, whose reading is not confined to murder stories, war reminiscences, pornography and, for real culture, the *Reader's Digest*.

But, if the ability and the wish to read is one of the distinguishing marks of today's, and, one hopes, tomorrow's uncommon man and if we are faced with the problem of the man with a good brain and a large job who has lost the habit of reading or has never acquired it, what can we propose in the way of suitable books? The question is better put, perhaps, by saying, 'suitable kinds of books', rather than 'suitable books', because to prescribe a reading list for an intelligent, responsible adult is almost as silly as advising such a person to eat only in this or that restaurant, visit only this or that hairdresser or wear this or that colour of tie. A large measure of personal choice is essential and half the value of the exercise lies in developing the ability to make a good choice, which must mean a choice which is suited to one's temperament and state of mind. To say, 'You ought to read this' is certainly arrogant and impertinent, and probably irrelevant as well, whereas 'I think this man writes well and has something to say, and I think you might enjoy his work and get something out of it' is more sensible and humane and stands a much better chance of success.

The following suggestions are made in the full knowledge of the fact that some readers are going to find them obvious, unnecessary and even patronising and that others will consider them upstage and impossibly ambitious. Over the past twenty years, however, a number of busy people of the type to which the present book is addressed have said they have found them useful, if only to argue about and disagree with, and they are consequently put forward with a fair amount of confidence.

1. Make it an unbreakable rule to spend at least half-an-hour a week browsing round in a bookshop which, ideally, does nothing but sell books, but in any case one in which the books are not just a sideline to the stationery, jigsaw puzzles, brass ornaments and greetings cards. Browsing, for those who are not familiar with the practice, means picking out any book which catches one's eye, noting the name of the author and reading his biography on the back flap, skimming through a few pages to get the flavour and then replacing it on the shelf.

2. Buy and read one book a week from a first-class firm of paperback publishers. Such a firm can be easily identified, because its books have no cover-pictures of nudes or near-nudes, girls in leather clothing or people of either

sex holding whips or guns. By rigorously avoiding the nudes, leather, whips or guns paperbacks, the inexperienced reader can at least avoid wasting his time on books which are worth nobody's time. He will, of course, make mistakes, but the first sifting will have been done for him and that, for a busy person, is a very great blessing. After twelve months getting one's bearings in this way, one can venture with greater confidence into the wider paperback market.

3. Make sure that at least one book in four is by a woman.

4. Try to maintain the proportion of biographies and autobiographies at a fairly high level.

5. Avoid treating your paperbacks as if they were magazines. Keep them to read again if the spirit moves you and as evidence of a year's reading. Write your name in each one, to make it clear to other people and to yourself that it is your own property and that it reflects a personal choice. Add the date when you bought it. This makes book-buying a morale-building series of encouraging occasions.

One of the biggest and saddest differences between homes of British and American executives on the one hand and continental executives, east and west of the Iron Curtain on the other, is the number of books one sees around. In general, the British and Americans have disgracefully few and the Germans, Poles, Scandinavians and the rest a considerable number. It cannot be a coincidence that – and again one is generalising – the Continental businessman tends to be a more interesting person to talk to and that he is much less likely to feel inferior and consequently to behave arrogantly in the company both of non-businessmen and of women.

Every businessman should hang a text in his bathroom, bedroom or some other suitable place, saying, in large letters: *MY BUSINESS IS BORING TO OTHER PEOPLE.* This is not, of course, necessarily true, but it can act as a constant reminder of the need both to keep oneself in good

mental training by having plenty of other things to talk about
and to learn to discuss one's business in a non-boring way.

REFERENCES

1. *The Times*, July 15, 1975.
2. *The Times*, July 15, 1975.

5. Nine case studies of effective and ineffective performers

'Mr Thompson,'[1] we wrote in our report to his employers, 'is an original. One would not easily take him for an industrial manager. He talks about his work in a way that suggests that his life is well-balanced, with plenty of things in it besides work. This, in our opinion, makes for the best kind of industrial spokesman, the man who can talk convincing sense about his employer's business, because he sees that business in its wider context.

'Visually, there is a Brian Rix quality about him and, for this reason, his words need to have an extra weight, which would not otherwise be necessary. Mr Thompson is fully aware of this.

'As a performer, he has the kind of throw-away charm which the immense success of Bertie Wooster and Lord Peter Wimsey proves goes down very well indeed with the British public. We would like to think that charm was on the increase in British industry, because, as well as being agreeable in itself, it has powerful commercial and political advantages, but regrettably our evidence goes the other way. We think you should congratulate yourselves on having Mr Thompson as a member of your staff.'

Mr Thompson, in his mid-forties, had an alive, humorous face. An accountant by training, he was not in the least surprised to hear us say that we would not have taken him for an accountant at all. 'You're confusing professional account-ants with company accountants,' he told us, 'and particularly with the kind of accountant we try to employ.' Professional accountants, it was explained to us, tended to look, dress and sound like solicitors, whereas accountants, or ex-accountants, working for industrial concerns were not the same sort of animal at all. He himself had been a member of the board for three years, took a keen interest in all the affairs of the company and had recently done a stint as Personnel Manager, with much enjoyment, while the real man was away recovering from an operation. He read a lot, played the violin for relaxation, and spent as much time as possible working in his large garden. He had gone for this company in the first place mainly because it had the reputation of being non-stuffy, but also because it was in a small country town. The thought of working in a big-city atmosphere was utterly repellent to him and, as he put it, 'I'd have to be starving to do it.'

He was, as we indicated in our report, an immensely attractive, successful speaker. His pleasantness made one anxious to hear what he had to say and he had that rare quality which is essential for the first-class communicator, the ability to make a listener feel that he is part of the occasion and that his responses would be watched for and welcomed. There was no trace of anxiety or tension in his manner, no worry about not saying the right thing, or using the wrong word. If one agreed with what he said, so much the better but, if not, there was no reason to bother. Life was to be enjoyed, not fretted about, and it was obvious that here was a fundamentally unsnobbish, unpretentious man, who took people as he found them, no matter what their rank or position.

Mr Birtwistle, alas, had few of Mr Thompson's advantages. In his mid-thirties, he had received rapid promotion in his family's well-known textile business and at the time we met him he was a member of the Board and in charge of the export side of the enterprise. He did not strike us as being particularly intelligent and we doubted very much if he would have found himself occupying such a responsible and well-paid job had he not belonged to the right family.

This, however, was a point we felt unable to make in writing and we accordingly contented ourselves with the following, which was truthful and may, with luck, have done some good, both to the firm and to the individual concerned.

'Mr Birtwistle took a considerable time to adjust himself to the group.[2] For the first hour or two, he did not appear to be particularly pleased to be spending the day with us and his answers to questions were somewhat brusque and mono-syllabic. Later, however, he became more talkative, and, although he never gave the impression of being enthusiastic about his work, he produced, under firm but, we hope, kindly questioning, some interesting items of information about the company and the industry.

'Neither we nor the other members of the group succeeded in discovering any leisure-time interests which he may have. It is possible that he considers these too personal or too unfashionable to be revealed to any but his own circle of intimate friends. He was at his most fluent and interesting when describing a recent summer holiday in Corsica, but, in any talk or interview he may give for public consumption he should be careful not to use phrases like, "We went in May to avoid the mob".

'We are sure he would benefit greatly from regular contact with people in less prosperous and secure circumstances than his own and probably also from one of the longer courses in a good business school, where he would find himself fully stretched for several hours each day.'

To use less diplomatic language, Mr Birtwistle was a dull, heavy man and we could frankly see no easy way of helping him to become anything different. One could not say that he was unpleasant. There was a certain bovine loveableness about him at times and he was capable of producing slightly off-beat comments about the textile industry, such as, 'I can't think what people used to do with all the cloth we used to make. I'm sure they didn't need it', which pleased the rest of the group and suggested that, had he felt so inclined, he could have developed a slow-moving, but fluent style, which would have suited his temperament and appearance and made him a good many friends.

The man who was actually offered to us, however, appeared to see no particular point in showing enthusiasm about his work or his life. He no doubt appreciated the advantages of being where he was, but he struck us as being hardly the person to do either his company or the industry a good turn by appearing in a broadcast programme about the prospects of textile manufacturing in Britain. He might possibly have made a reasonably satisfactory production controller, or even an accountant, of the plodding type, but, as things were, there was a disastrous contradiction between his manner and his selling function in the company. One could not believe that he was in the appropriate job, and, even worse, there was a feeling in one's mind that Mr Birtwistle had much the same doubts about himself.

With better luck and no doubt a more satisfactory parentage and upbringing, Mr Birtwistle might have become quite an appealing kind of eccentric, instead of a disgruntled misfit. Mentally, we contrasted him with one of our previous clients, a prosperous farmer from the Welsh borders, Mr Pratt. Mr Pratt, as large and heavy a man as Mr Birtwistle, was certainly no beauty and, in looks, this friendly, self-assured, humorous character was as rural as they come. His family had owned and run the farm for generations and our Mr Pratt, like his father before him, took a very active interest in agricultural politics, at the local, national and, more recently, international levels. He was, as we pointed out to him, exceptionally well suited to EEC negotiations and fact-finding tours, since he had, in the words of our report, 'a physical appearance very frequently found among farmers in Belgium and the north of France. In this sense,' we went on, 'he is not only farming personified, but Common Market farming personified, and we hope the National Farmers' Union recognises and values this asset.'

His looks, however, were by no means his only asset. 'He

has,' we pointed out, 'extraordinary political skill in parrying direct and possibly embarrassing questions and in making the kind of improbable and unprovable statements, such as: "The price of meat is bound to come down", which knock the wind out of an interviewer. In all this he is greatly helped by his Welsh accent and by his talent for talking like a small farmer when he is in fact a very large farmer.'

'His powers of farming gamesmanship,' we concluded, 'are probably unbeatable.'

There was no doubt that much of Mr Pratt's great success as a public figure stemmed from his independent spirit and his massive confidence, which must in turn have been the products of an ample income; of being in complete control of one's own successful business, with no irritations like shareholders, Boards or ambitious colleagues to bother about; and of something as close to security as our frenzied and unsettled age offers. His manner was likely to suggest to everyone, British or foreign, with whom he came into contact that here was a man who was good at his job and who was afraid of nothing and of nobody. The thought of anyone breathing down Mr Pratt's neck was ludicrous.

A special aspect of his strength – and this is true of all good speakers – was the impression he gave of having plenty in reserve. For every piece of information he produced, and for every throw-away remark, one was sure he had half-a-dozen waiting ready in the wings. There was a vast authority about him, although one realised after a while that a fair proportion of his *ex cathedra* statements were not meant to be taken too seriously. It was in fact his delicious talent for mingling fact and fancy and of gently playing with his audience which made one feel that one was dealing with a master at the game. Possibly owing to the half-Welsh environment in which he lived, talking was obviously a great pleasure to him and his pleasure was infectious. He had for some years been in demand for television and radio. Our comment on this was: 'Mr Pratt can be safely entrusted with any broadcasting occasion known to us.' This, to anyone who had met him and seen him in action was a judgement which required no great degree of insight or imagination.

In our experience, farmers and the headquarters staff of the National Farmers' Union for the most part make good public performers. The reason for this is not far to seek. Their work is concerned with the basic reality of providing their fellow citizens with food. Unlike the promoters of pop records, cigarettes and pet foods, they are unlikely to lie awake at night wondering if they are earning a living producing irrelevancies, absurdities and confidence tricks. It is easier to sound convincing if one is talking about things that people really need.

Where there is a weakness among people who are spokesmen for the agricultural industry, it generally arises from a life characterised by too much farming and too little broad human contact. The result is that specialised knowledge is not put across in a way that the general public understands or sympathises with.

This emerged in a slightly different way with Mr Greening. Mr Greening was, and presumably still is, a thoroughly likeable person – patient, kindly and clear thinking. We stress this fact deliberately, before saying what his job was – a Regional Controller for the Post Office. The Post Office unfortunately has a bad image nowadays. It is commonly regarded, with some justice, as inefficient, unimaginative and lacking in courage, so that to label one of its high-ranking officials as 'clear-thinking' may cause disbelief here and there. Every organisation, however, the Post Office included, contains people who are better than it deserves and Mr Greening may well have been such a person. It is equally possible, on the other hand, that the Post Office employs a great many extremely able and conscientious men, who are constantly frustrated by the idiotic policy limits within which they have to function. To lay all the misdeeds and failings of the Post Office at Mr Greening's door would be extremely unfair, but the Post Office, none the less, has a certain widely held public image and Mr Greening failed to correspond to that image. One needed a little time to adjust oneself to the fact that here was a man who departed widely from the stereotype.

His qualities, we felt, 'must be of great value to him in what is probably a pretty lonely job. During the two days he was with us, he absorbed our suggestions and criticisms in the most encouraging way and was always glad to come back at us with points of his own.

'Although he is obviously the most loyal and tactful of public servants', we went on, 'we think the Post Office could help him and his fellow-executives in two important ways, both of which would, in our opinion, increase their managerial efficiency and improve their morale:

a. By increasing the frequency of their regular contacts with London and with their regional colleagues at the same level as themselves. Memos and telephone conversations are not an adequate substitute for regular and preferably informal personal meetings.
b. By a strong, continuous, aggressive and truthful campaign to explain to the public the problems the Post Office is facing and the ways in which it proposes to solve them. Regional staff cannot do this on their own and it is unreasonable to expect them to.'

The second of these recommendations is dealt with in greater detail in a later section. Here it seems necessary to point out only that men in Mr Greening's position are those who have to be in direct contact with the customers every day of their working life. These are the people the local newspapers, BBC and IBA are always wanting to interview and the people who are asked to take part in consumer brains trusts and to talk to Rotary and Townswomen's Guilds. They are the Post Office, British Rail, Gas and Electricity to the residents of Birmingham, Cardiff and Liverpool. They are, in commercial parlance, the point-of-sale people and no manufacturer in his right mind would expect his salesmen to function without a carefully thought out advertising campaign – and in these days of economic depression the nationalised industries need to sell as hard as anybody. The absence of such a campaign puts the local man in an impossible position. He has to do headquarters' job and his own at the same time, not infrequently with only half the information he needs. If Mr Greening, despite all his ability and charm, sometimes sounded a little unconvincing to us when presenting the Post Office case, the root of his trouble was undoubtedly that he was having to function as a field commander who has either had no communication with his political and military masters for weeks or who is trying to do sensible things locally in the knowledge that these same masters have been seriously insane for some time. It is not the best foundation for a resounding public appearance, however gifted a performer one may happen to be and one can easily understand that first-class people may, on occasion, give the impression that their heart is not wholly in what they are saying.

Dr Beeston, head of the Economics Department in what we had better call for safety merely a large British company, gave his listeners no reason to believe that he had a heart at all, either in or out of what he was saying. In his early forties, he was dark, handsome in a saturnine, rather frightening way, and made it abundantly clear that, in attending the course, he had been compelled by his employers to spend two days slumming. To say that he did not get on with his fellow students was a massive understatement. They soon came to dislike him very much indeed, and with good reason. 'Dr Beeston', we wrote afterwards, and with all the diplomacy we could muster, 'found it difficult to adjust to the group, all of whom were earning at least his own salary, and to whom he had no reason that we could see to feel superior.'

But superior Dr Beeston undoubtedly did feel, and if this is his attitude to us, we wondered modestly, whatever would he be like on television, in front of a cross-section of the

British people? An answer of sorts came incidentally from
Dr Beeston himself. It appeared that he had twice been
interviewed on television, 'and on neither occasion did I find
it an enjoyable experience'. One has a duty to dig below the
surface when something in a man's attitude to life creates
such an unfortunate barrier between him and his audience,
and eventually we found a clue.

It is often useful, as a mind-loosener, to ask a highly-
trained specialist this type of question: 'Are you a Krupps
man who happens at the moment to be working with com-
puters, or a computer man who happens at the moment to
be working for Krupps?' Most people answer this without
hesitation and the exercise sorts them out into two piles,
those whose primary loyalty is to the company and those who
put the speciality first, with the company largely an accident.
Dr Beeston produced his reply almost before we had finished
the question: he was an economist who happened at that
moment to be working for that particular large British company, and there was no doubt in his mind as to who was
conferring a benefit on whom.

This made the situation much clearer. The man in front
of us was an economist whose heart was in the academic world,
not in the industry which provided him with a very good
living. Given half a chance, he would be out and away to an
academic job without the slightest hesitation, and meanwhile
he had to prove his fitness and worthiness for such an opportunity by not bringing himself down to the level of mere
businessmen, or, for that matter, mere members of the public.
In a gathering of what he would have thought of as fellow-
academics, he might possibly have dropped this pose and
become more of a human being, or rather that special breed
of humanity, an academic human being.

The man we had to deal with was pompous, condescending
and quite unable, or maybe unwilling, to talk in an ordinary
conversational way. It was not merely that he paraded his
technical jargon in a manner that was irritating, rather than
funny. We recalled a previous economist, who held a uni-

versity chair in the subject, who had referred to himself as being 'temporarily short of liquidity', when all that was meant was that he had come out without any cash on him. This, however, was a much more lovable character, and his strange language was well taken, as it normally is if the person who produces it shows a reasonable amount of warmth and friend-liness. The main trouble with Dr Beeston, however, was not his technicalities, but his insistence on qualifying everything he said. Nothing could be allowed to remain simple or straight-forward, to have done so would have amounted to professional treason of the worst kind. For Dr Beeston, there were no such things as 'Yes', 'No', and 'I think so'. Plain statements like 'That couldn't possibly work', or 'I'm sure that would be the best way of going about it' never came from him. He was *homo academicus* and for him the plain, unqualified statement was proof of an inferior, untrained mind.

Our report on him ended with these, we hope, constructive words. 'Dr Beeston, we are sure, is well-fitted to run an important research department. His speaking style, however, to which he obviously attaches great value, acts as a barrier between him and the general public, and during the short period he was with us we were unable to persuade him to modify it in any way.'

We did, on the contrary, make considerable progress with Mrs Leaf. She was in her late fifties, and worked as a full-time Regional Officer for an international peace organisation, a job which involved a great many speaking engagements with a wide range of audiences. A vigorous, cheerful woman, she recorded on her preliminary assessment form that she felt she had become 'more confident, tolerant and understanding' during the past ten years or so and believed that this improve-ment had been brought about by her job and by 'adversity in private life'. Her voice she described as 'soft' and she considered that she had 'no pronounced accent'. So far as she was aware, her only mannerism was 'a nervous movement of the hands and fingers'.

An objective observer could have fairly summed up Mrs Leaf by saying that she 'was of ladylike manner and appearance'. One meets many women of similar type – a very agreeable and impressive type – as headmistresses, personnel officers and on the upper levels of the Civil Service. It is the executive variety of the English gentlewoman and it is probably, alas, on the way out, as more socially neutral figures push their way up from below. Mrs Leaf's successors will probably describe their personal misfortunes in less reticent terms than 'adversity in private life' and their voices may well not be 'soft'. They will certainly demand more money than a member of her generation has been prepared to accept.

It was not true that she had 'no pronounced accent'. As any working-class person could have told her, she sounded unmistakably like a member of the class from which she came. There was nothing regional about her voice, no trace of Scots, Welsh or the North, but everything about her said, 'I had a comfortable, gentle upbringing, I went to a good school and I have the ideas and values of the layer of society into which I was born. I know all these things are unfashionable nowadays and I realise that people with my kind of background are being taxed, pushed and hated out of existence. But I am trying to do the best I can for society with the only equipment I have.'

Her problem, if one can put it that way, was that she was conscious of a certain and probably increasing amount of difficulty in getting her excellent ideas across to people, especially young people, whose background, habits and pattern of thinking were very different from her own. What, she wanted to know, could be done about this?

We listened to her in action and noted three characteristics which, singly and together, might well be the source of the trouble. The first was that Mrs Leaf did quite unmistakably belong to yesterday's upper layer of British society. The second was a slightly over-formal manner. And the third was a failure to approach the audience as a person: she practically never said 'I'. We felt, and told her, that if she concentrated

on the third of these, the other two would more or less correct themselves, or at least become much less noticeable.

This piece of advice applies to many more people than Mrs
Leaf, men as well as women. The therapy is simple. It involves
no more than remembering that one's talk has to be presented
in terms of: 'I remember one day – it must have been about
three years ago – I was talking to a retired general and he said
to me . . .' and not of, 'Many retired military men are of the
opinion that . . .' The first method brings an audience into
touch with a real person, the second leaves the speaker shadowy, which is always a disadvantage, because, baulked of the
chance to meet an actual man or woman, the members of an
audience are left free to create a fantasy one from the scraps
of evidence their imagination is supplied with to feed on.
Unless they are given good reasons to believe the contrary,
they will conclude from Mrs Leaf's upper-crust accent, her
gentle, non-aggressive manner, her fluency, her frequent
use of 'one' and her non-conversational style, that the woman
they are listening to and looking at belongs to a world which
is not theirs. Once this happens, her ideas, too, are likely to
be dismissed as intellectual, old-fashioned and irrelevant.

We convinced Mrs Leaf of this and, so long as she was with
us, disciplined her to see and present life in an 'I' form. In
one sense this was easy for her – she had plenty of experiences
to draw on – but in another it was very difficult – her training,
from the time she was a small girl, had caused her instinctively
to shy away from 'I' and 'me'. For her, 'I' was a person to
be kept well in the background. Politeness and decency
demanded 'one would think, wouldn't one?', or 'It's usual to
feel, isn't it?', not 'I'm a strong believer in . . .', but the impact
of the 'I' sentence is several times stronger than the others
and, equally important, the 'I' approach is much more difficult to contradict. Personal experiences actually happened,
and, short of calling the speaker a liar, an audience has to
accept them, but to 'It's usual to feel, isn't it?' the answer that
follows can be 'no' just as easily as 'yes'.

Once one has said 'I', one's personal peculiarities fall into

place. They are simply, take them or leave them, part of 'I'.
Without the 'I', the peculiarities steal the scene, and an
audience gives its whole attention to them, to the exclusion of
all else. Mrs Leaf said she was extremely grateful for the
information and promised to do her best to overcome her
inhibitions and to try hard to put our advice into practice.

So, too, did Mr Tanner, although he, assuredly, had no
upper-class background to weigh him down. Forty-five and a
successful marketing manager, he used up some of his spare
energy in various forms of public work – a county councillor,
a magistrate and a school governor. His ambitions, it was
probably fair to say, were much more in the field of his
unpaid activities than in his marketing. This, one felt, was a
man who was destined to come into full flower from the age of
fifty onwards and whose present efforts were devoted mainly
to preparing him for that stage in his life. To become chairman of the council and of the bench by the time he was fifty
was probably his dream, and being a Member of Parliament
was by no means ruled out.

Meanwhile, he felt that he had two weaknesses as a public
performer and he was anxious to get rid of them. The first
was that he spoke too fluently and, to use his own phrase,
sounded glib as a result, and the second was that he was 'a
poor listener', with no great interest in what the other man
was thinking. To fulfil his ambitions in a really successful
way, he ought, he felt, to sound more solid, more reflective,
more philosophical, less like the good salesman he was. This
meant, we suggested, that he wanted to slow himself down or,
at least, to give the impression of having slowed himself
down, and we went on to explain what the difference was.
An Italian, to an English ear, appears to be talking very fast,
partly because the language he is using is unfamiliar, or
possibly incomprehensible, and partly because Italian has a
large proportion of polysyllabic words, which means that, in
order to convey the same meaning as an Englishman, an
Italian has to employ many more syllables, most of which

will be touched quickly and lightly. An Italian trips along, so to speak, and an Englishman has a more measured tread. He is not actually talking faster, but he sounds as if he is. Speed in speech is a very subjective affair.

It is, in fact, extremely difficult to get a naturally rapid speaker to utter his sentences more slowly. To do this would mean changing the pattern and tempo of his mind and to cause a very serious degree of frustration. The fast talker is normally the fast thinker and to attempt to slow him down is, in a sense, to destroy him. What one can do, however, and without the slightest damage to his personality, is to teach such a person the value of a calculated, well-timed pausing.

Suppose, for instance, that we have this short passage:

> I was sitting on the seat in the sunshine, (A) just watching people walking by, (A) and I noticed an extraordinary looking man coming across the grass towards me. (B) He must have been well over seven feet tall and in his right hand he had something one doesn't often see nowadays, (A) a large butter-fly net. (B) He came over to the seat where I was, sat down at the other end of it and took something unbelievable out of a haversack he had over his shoulder (B) – a very small monkey, which perched on his shoulder as soon as he let it out.

It is possible to speak it continuously and at an even pace of, say, 150 words a minute. If one does this, one's listeners will certainly feel that they are dealing with someone who talks very fast. But, if one pauses for a count of one at the points marked (A) and of two at the points marked (B), the effect is entirely different. Spoken without these pauses, the passage lasts for approximately 40 seconds, and with the pauses for another 9 seconds. There need be no slowing down while one is actually speaking – the full 150 words a minute rate can be maintained – but the inclusion of the pauses not only gives the listener a chance to understand and absorb what is being said to him but changes the overall pace of the speaker's delivery in a fundamental way. He automatically sounds more

reasonable, more considerate, less anxious to be finished and
gone, more interested in his audience, more mellow and
reflective, all the things which Mr Tanner was so eager to
achieve for himself. With someone of his intelligence, there
was no great difficulty in developing the habit of counting
one for a comma and two for a full stop, or its equivalent,
and one has only to play the recording of the same passage
with and without pauses for the beneficial result to be immediately apparent.

What impressed Mr Tanner so much was the extra weight
the pauses gave him. A man who was previously only eloquent
and quick-witted – glib was the term he used – had transformed himself, at least superficially, into someone of quite a
different status, a fitting chairman of the County Council and
the Bench, in fact. We say 'at least superficially', because we
remained somewhat doubtful of the quality of Mr Tanner's
mental cargo. He was an excellent talker, in the sense that he
was never at a loss for a word and that he could be relied on
to keep going, come what may, but what he had to say was not
of any great profundity. His life had been essentially one of
movement and activity, of doing things, rather than reflecting
on things. His first-hand experience had been fairly narrow
and, so far as we could discover, he had never given himself
the opportunity to broaden himself through reading. He
showed great skill in concealing this, but he was vulnerable
under pressure from someone who was determined to find out
how much he really knew and if that pressure was maintained
he could lose something of his calm and confidence. In the
circumstances we thought he was quite right in deciding to
go for a technique which would make him sound wiser and
better equipped than he actually was. He had, incidentally, a
very good ear, and adapted his original Yorkshire accent well
to the company in which he found himself. His own assessment of this was interesting. 'The north country origin of
my parents', he wrote, 'occasionally pokes through a not
very thick public school overlay.' He might have added,
'when I allow it to'.

Mr Cherrill, our next example, though he had 'a quiet, rather formal BBC voice, with a tendency to trail away at the end of sentences'. His most irritating mannerism, he believed, was 'a tendency to repeat "you know" '. As often happens, this supposed blemish failed to show up during the period when Mr Cherrill was with us, possibly for the same reason that an aching tooth so often stops aching at the dentist's door: the greater fear drives out the lesser.

A Cambridge engineering graduate in his early forties, Mr Cherrill occupied a high technical post in one of the nationalised industries. This very pleasant, gentle and courteous man had, when we first met him, what we described in our report as 'a rather formal and slightly over-cautious manner, frequently found, in our experience, with technical people'. As the course proceeded, 'he gradually loosened up and by the second day he was expressing himself much more easily and effectively'.

This, we concluded, was 'a man who benefits very much from the opportunity to talk to people with a different kind of expertise from his own. We had the impression that part of his early stiffness was due to an over-narrow working, and possibly social environment, and to his lack of experience in seeing himself and his job in a wider context. If he could be encouraged to and maybe helped to move out of his professional field a little more, we think his employers would gain a good deal and that he himself would develop a more expansive technique in dealing with other people. We found him a most likeable and obviously competent man, who is more modest than he needs to be.'

At this point it may be useful to fill in a little more of Mr Cherrill's background. His father had been a doctor and his mother came of a long line of clergymen, one of whom was a mid-Victorian bishop. He had been brought up in a cultured atmosphere and his choice of engineering rather than medicine, as a career did not altogether meet with his family's approval. His good degree and successful research – he had acquired the all-important doctorate which allowed him to be called by the same title as his father – and his subsequent career had done something to improve his mother's and father's view of engineering as a suitable occupation for their son, but the struggle had left him with a certain feeling of guilt and with a diffidence of manner which, although by no means unattractive in conversation, was a disadvantage at meetings and in speaking to general audiences. One had the feeling that here was a man who did not fully believe in himself, an impression which was intensified by his habit of letting his voice die away towards the end of sentences, as if he had lost interest half way through in what he was saying.

This was not the only explanation, however. Mr Cherrill had a great fear of boring people and of invading their mental privacy. It would occur to him after he had begun to say something that perhaps other people might not be in the least interested in the thoughts that were forming themselves in his mind and that it would be impolite and tedious to go on. We suspected, perhaps wrongly, that either his father or his mother, or possibly both, had overwhelmed him with their own ideas when he was a child and that, having suffered in this way, he had become determined not to inflict similar torment on other people. He was sensitive about what he called his BBC voice for the same reason; some of his listeners might find it offensive and so he had no right to inflict it on them.

Mr Cherrill belonged to that large group of people whose morale suffers without a daily dose of praise and encouragement. He was not sufficiently sure of himself to be able to thrive unless he had the clearly expressed approval of the men and women with whom he came into daily contact. When this came his way, as it did during his two days with us, he emerged from his shell, his languor disappeared and he became animated to a degree that showed what was bottled up inside him.

One should make a clear distinction between Mr Cherrill's principal symptom, fading away, and that dreadful plague among speakers, falling tones. Sufferers from falling tones drop their voice at every comma and full stop, and the effect is to make them sound miserable and self-pitying. The complaint is most common among women, particularly educated women between the ages of 25 and 50. It is no doubt to some extent a fashion and infectious, but it also has deep personal roots, as if the speaker were trying to say to the world: 'I'm really a very intelligent person. For the past 5, 10, 20 years I've been taken out of circulation, chained to the kitchen sink, and prevented from using my talents. I intend to show society through the tone in my voice, what I've suffered.' There is very little that an outsider can do to help anyone in this position, except to point out that the public usually resents having to listen to people who sound miserable and the falling-tone symptom rarely brings the sympathy and understanding that are longed for so much.

Mrs Williamson was the very opposite of a falling-tone woman. A product of Cheltenham Ladies' College and an Oxford graduate, she had nine successful years in the Civil Service before she married herself off at 30, to an architect in a good way of business. In the determined and I-know-exactly-what-I'm-doing style that was typical of her, she then proceeded to have three children in four years and, with that little matter out of the way, began to lay the foundations of a political career. At 40 she was well on the road, as a candidate at the General Election – a Conservative candidate, it is important to mention – and not long afterwards, with another General Election in the offing, she had been adopted for a much more promising constituency, which she believed, rightly as it turned out, that she had every chance of winning.

Blonde, bursting with energy, and immensely confident and cheerful, she might have appeared to be the last person to need any advice from anybody, but she, too, had her worries, as it turned out. The new-style Conservative Member, the future Minister of the 1980s, ought not, she felt, to sound exactly like her. Didn't we agree that people might find her just a little too obviously prosperous, CLC and Oxford? Her appearance, she thought, was probably a trifle on the garden-party side, but she could cope satisfactorily with that on her own, she was sure.

At the root of Mrs Williamson's need for assistance was the unchangeable fact that the constituency she was planning – Mrs Williamson always planned, rather than hoped – to win was socially very mixed, one of the curious Midlands blends of industry and expensive executive suburbs. Very sensibly, she wanted to be equally acceptable to both and, indeed, to win the seat she had to be. The willingness was obviously there and the question then became two questions. 'How accurately do you hear and see yourself?' and 'How good an actress are you?'

The first of these questions was easily dealt with. We simply played recordings, sound and pictures, back to her to find out if she reacted in the way we did and, on the whole, the answer was that she did not. The image was too far to the political right and too upstage for any ambitious politician's peace of mind in the 1970s and much more so than she realised, and most of the trouble arose from the way she talked. We asked her to notice these significant differences between the style of the top 10 per cent of the British people – a very small proportion of her constituents, however vocal and influential it might be – and the rest. We called them, very unscientifically but, we thought, meaningfully, Group A and Group B, and we put the differences under four heads.

1. *Loudness of voice.*   Group A tends to speak as if the whole of the rest of the world were deaf and had failed to equip itself with a hearing aid. This is a curious class habit and it appears to be of long standing, possibly going back to ear-trumpet days and to the constant presence of elderly relatives in the household. It infuriates lesser mortals, especially when it happens in shops, restaurants and other public places. Group A conversations are rarely private in the ordinary sense of the word; they are intended to be heard by all and sundry. This remarkable custom may well have something to do with long years spent in boarding-

schools, where there is no dividing line between private and public life. Mrs Williamson had Group A loudness.

2. *Over-stressing*, *combined with heaven-soaring*.   This well-known feature of Group A speech is not always recognised for what it is – putting an altogether ridiculous and unnecessary emphasis on totally unimportant words and syllables. It has been usefully called the How Absolutely Marvellous syndrome, from the Group A habit of coming down on *Ab* and *Mar* with both feet at the beginning of the syllable and then jumping up to the skies at the end. Mrs Williamson had over-stressing and heaven-soaring to a very marked extent.

3. *The One disease*.   'One shouldn't do that, should one?' This is entirely a Group A characteristic and possibly the most certain class-label in Britain. Mrs Williamson had the One disease.

4. *Certain hunt-ball vowels*.   Especially *o*s and *a*s. Mrs Williamson went to Crawss-in-Hend with the best of them.

In her position, as a prospective Conservative MP, we felt that *3* and *4* were much less serious than *1* and *2*. Had she been aiming at a Labour seat, something drastic and urgent would have had to be done about *1*, *2*, *3* and *4*, but no Member of Parliament, of whatever colour, nowadays can expect to get away with *1* and *2*. These two diseases are not, in fact, all that difficult to cure. We advised Mrs Williamson to adopt as her professional motto the words *calm down*. Interpreted in more practical terms, this meant: try to talk more quietly; stress only those syllables which deserve a stress; and remember that most people have reasonably good hearing. We also thought it would do her good to have as many conversations as possible – not just polite exchanges of greetings – with people who had a different kind of social background from her own, and who spoke in a less high-powered fashion and on another tune.

Mrs Williamson is now a Member of Parliament. It would

be immodest, and probably incorrect, to suggest that such a happy outcome is the result of following our advice.

The nine case studies described above do no more than illustrate the wide range of problems which face men and women at the executive level when they have the task of putting their ideas across in public. It may be comforting, we hope it is, to discover that other people experience the same difficulties as one has oneself, and the remedies we proposed to our clients could certainly be more widely useful. The point to emphasise above all others, however, is that one can do no more than analyse the problem to the best of one's ability and then to make certain suggestions which the patient may or may not feel inclined to take up. In the long run, self-analysis and the ability to see and hear oneself from outside is what matters, and this means self-analysis all the time and on every occasion. Some people enjoy this and improve; others find it unpleasant or disturbing, and prefer to stay as they are. It is and must be a personal choice.

NOTES

1. Throughout this chapter all names are fictitious and we have made certain other small modifications here and there, to remove all clues to the man or his employers.
2. These groups were limited to six people, and it was rare to have more than two people from the same organisation within a group. In Mr. Birtwistle's case he was the sole representative of his company.

6. The businessman and the media

'We have to improve and refine our methods', said the Vice-Chancellor of a certain university on a public occasion recently, 'in order that more students can be processed through the available resources.' The Vice-Chancellor is reported to have been surprised at the way in which this, as he thought, inoffensive remark was seized on by what are nowadays called, in the jargon phrase, the media. The University's Public Relations Officer did his best to explain that all the Vice-Chancellor meant was that in these hard times students had to be taught more efficiently and that it was the University's business to discover ways of doing this. The media were not satisfied. The sentence was widely quoted, with the implication that this particular university, if not the whole academic world, was a pretty inhumane, impersonal affair, with raw students going in at one end of the machine and graduates coming out at the other, which appeared to correspond quite closely with the views of at least part of the national student body.

Public men may complain of misrepresentation, of sensationalism, of ignorance, of vindictiveness, and of many other failings of which the press and broadcasting people are frequently accused. The criticism may well be justified, but the sad fact is that the media exist and that somehow one has to live with them and, if need be, defend oneself against them. This particular Vice-Chancellor's dislike and suspicion of reporters and interviewers is well known in the part of the country in which he functions. He is a shy man, who is happiest well away from the limelight, which is bound to make a disinterested observer wonder if the right person was appointed to the job. Other university administrators are much fonder of public appearances and leap at the opportunity to hit the headlines, or to propose or defend something on television, reckoning that the old adage about any news being good news is correct and that personal advancement, especially in the title-hungry Britain, the coveted knight-hood, is likely to happen sooner rather than later if one becomes well-known to the general public. In the matter of publicity, as of all other things, one man's meat is indeed another man's poison.

Anyone who is likely to have come into regular contact with reporters or editors ought, as a matter of prudence, to be well informed about the kind of people they are and the condi-tions under which they work. Many public figures, actual or in the making, are surprisingly ignorant about these matters, and a little clarification and explanation might be helpful.

The first necessity is to make a distinction between those stories (the term is a technical one and much despised by many people who find themselves the subject of a journalist's 'story') which have to be produced at great speed and those which are not tied to a particular hour or a particular day. All journalists have tales to tell of important men who expect to see the draft of a story before it is published and who are astounded and enraged to hear that nothing of the kind is possible, since their copy is already in the hands of the printer and will be on the news-stands in a couple of hours' time. Phrases like 'I demand' are a common feature of editors' lives, and, although the editor rarely says anything that amounts to 'I refuse', the result is the same. The story appears in the way the paper has decided, the central figure has not seen it in advance, and there is usually absolutely nothing he can do about it.

This does not mean that newspapers are not responsive to pressure. All local newspapermen have to live and continue to work in a community, and some of the citizens in the community are more powerful than others. Stories involving prominent local people and members of their families are not infrequently suppressed altogether or rewritten to present the circumstances in a more favourable light. This happens particularly with the reporting of court cases and of impending business deals, which the reporter has come to hear about, but which, either by instinct or by acting on instructions, he decides to tuck away in the back of his mind and do nothing more about at the moment. A comparison between the news presented in both local and national newspapers, and in that invaluable window on British life, *Private Eye*, which does not suffer from such inhibitions, will make the point, without any need for further comment here.

Newspapers, however, have their favourites and their Aunt Sallies, and so do radio and television journalists. It would certainly not be true to say that any prominent local person can count on privileged and understanding treatment from the media, and an essential first step on the road to self-protection is to develop an accurate sense of the prejudices and assumptions of local journalists, who are, it is worth pointing out, working for the *Newtown Newsdesk*, not for *The Times* or the *Financial Times*, and for the mini-budget regional television magazine, not the plutocratic *Panorama*, with its generously allocated staff of all the talents.

Local journalists, whether they are reporters, sub-editors or editors, and whether they work with print, television cameras or microphones, will almost invariably have the attitudes and values of the *Sun* and the *Mirror*, not the *Guardian*, *The Times*, or even the *Telegraph*, a fact which is too often overlooked by people who themselves read the quality, rather than the popular press. This means that almost any story will be written and edited in the way which is calculated to please bus-drivers, assembly-workers and waitresses, who are numerous, rather than bank managers, marketing directors and bishops, who are relatively few. One says deliberately 'is calculated to please', because even journalists can make serious errors of judgement and may have failed to

notice significant changes in public taste and interest. Local
papers are not famous for their adventurous or pioneering
spirit and rely for the most part on the well-tried recipes
which have kept the books balanced for many years. Each
local newspaper area has its own sacred cows, and it is prudent
to be aware of them, if not to respect them. In Bristol, for
instance, the sacred cow is Concorde, which may never be
criticised. This aeroplane, with its record-breaking thirst for
public money, is assumed to be wholly in the interests of the
district, the nation and mankind. Its opponents are either
criminals or fools, and no holds are barred in dealing with
them. In Birmingham and Coventry the sacred cow is the
motor industry. To suggest, however mildly and tentatively,
that it should be encouraged to contract or perhaps to disappear, or that cars made by British Leyland are inferior to
those made by Toyota or Renault, would be to incur the
certain wrath of every right-thinking Midland newspaper.
Whatever their private opinions may be, in his working
hours every South Wales journalist is a public relations
officer for Welsh steel-making, every Midlands journalist for
car-making and every East Anglian journalist for large-scale
arable farming. Newly-established industries, or those which
do not fit into the ancient pattern are not likely to receive the
same super-friendly treatment. A large international petro-
chemical concern, which was contemplating a new plant
and an investment of several million pounds in the West
Country, was firmly told to go about its business by the
leader-writer of the local paper, on the grounds that it was
capital-intensive, not labour-intensive. Factories employing
a lot of people on simple manual tasks were one thing, but a
round-the-clock plant, with only a few skilled men to look
after it, was quite another matter and clearly the work of the
Devil. The fact that it was much less likely to close down
than the usual kind of local factory, with its low investment
per worker, made no more appeal than a plea for the British
Aircraft Corporation's works to be turned over to making
pre-fabricated housing would in Bristol.

The first rule, then, for any businessman inside or outside London must be to study the fixed ideas of his local paper and to read one or two of the popular national dailies and Sundays analytically and fairly regularly. This will prove of great value, not only in forecasting what line a particular paper is likely to take in connexion with one's firm or industry, but also in dealing with the broadcasting organisations, especially at regional level. Too few people realise that the radio or television journalist's day begins, usually at about ten o'clock, with a look through the morning papers, to discover stories which might be taken a little further through the day, and made into items for the early evening news bulletin or magazine programme. It is rare for a regional reporter employed by either the BBC or IBA to originate a story. He prefers to take over where the local or national paper has left off, partly because it is easier that way, partly because he is not allowed sufficient time to ferret out stories himself, and partly because his employer's lawyers find it safer. Anything that has already been published by someone else is less likely to cause legal complications if the story turns out to be wrong, misleading or for some other reason hot to hold. Since it is equally rare for anyone to be recruited as a broadcasting journalist without first having had a newspaper training, one can say without much fear of exaggeration that most of the journalists a businessman is likely to meet will think that the same things are important and the same things unimportant, in the jumble of material that constitutes the day's news.

The quality of journalists, like the quality of people in any other profession, is extremely variable. It has always been said that the better men and women tend to go to London, but before one accepts or rejects this it is necessary to define 'better'. A Mercedes or a Rolls Royce may be 'better' if one wants to travel from Hamburg to Nice in great comfort, but it is unquestionably worse than a Mini at threading its way along narrow lanes or at inching its way into a small suburban garage. One has to ask, 'better for what?' When one bears in mind the very high cost of living in London, the average provincial journalist of 40 or 50 probably does as well, in real money terms, as his colleage in Fleet Street. The people who make the pilgrimage to London, however, see themselves, not as average journalists in the making, but as exceptional journalists in the making. Their dream, in so far as journalists allow themselves to have dreams, is of becoming Industrial Editor of the *Guardian*, City Editor of the *Telegraph* or Foreign Editor of the *Express*. They want to specialise and, with supreme luck, to end up as Editor of the paper.

Most people in responsible jobs would prefer to deal with a specialist, rather than a general reporter. This is understandable, since the specialist has an accumulated body of knowledge and experience related to the subject in question. One does not have to start explaining everything to him as if he knew practically nothing already. The Educational Correspondent is expected to be up-to-date and well-informed on educational matters, the Agricultural Correspondent on farming and the Science Correspondent on science and technology. These experts are not, however, always as expert as their title might suggest. Some have been at it for years and others may be distinctly green. Every Industrial Correspondent has to start sometime and it may be one's bad luck to be confronted with him during his first week. In broadcasting, where changes of personnel are more widely noticed, there are reporters who have changed specialities more than once during the past ten years or so. The BBC's present Tokyo Correspondent, for instance, was formerly the Corporation's Educational Correspondent and not long before that its Home Affairs Correspondent. The last but one Court Correspondent moved into that prestigious post after gaining a well-deserved reputation for his football commentaries. The good general reporter is a very necessary member of any editor's staff and one can, as a member of the public, get much better results from him by appreciating his problems. If he has been in the district a long time, he will certainly have a wide knowledge of its characteristics and personalities as a whole, but there is no reason to suppose that he knows anything at all about the achievements or the difficulties of any particular concern within the area over which he is supposed to maintain a close watching brief. He may or may not understand what the new machine does or why the closure of a branch factory is unavoidable. The briefing which sent him on the job may have been inadequate or, quite possibly, entirely wrong. There is every likelihood that he will not need to come again for months or years. His previous assignment may have been to interview a pop star visiting the town, to look at the results of a big fire at a department store or to collect the names of the prizewinners at a horse-show. He will almost certainly be in a hurry and grateful for a quick rundown on the story as the firm sees it. He may or may not have a photographer with him.

What he is looking for is information which will allow him to write a paragraph or two of the kind which is likely to interest the bus-driver, waitress and small shop-keeper who are never far from his thoughts. This means one or two impressive facts, a short quote from someone in authority and, if possible, a superlative. Anything which is the biggest, thinnest, lightest, oldest, cheapest provides a good reason for writing the piece at all and gives a useful lead to the sub-editor who will write the headline. When one is being interviewed by a newspaper man, either face-to-face or on the telephone, one should ask oneself : 'what is it about me, this process, this strike which can be made to brighten the life of this very bored and cynical man just a little? What colour and sparkle can I find for him in the story?' Much of this spadework may just possibly have been already done by the company's efficient and imaginative public relations department, and the reporter may appear clutching a copy of that department's handout, with key words and phrases encouragingly underlined in the office before he set out on his rounds. It is equally likely, alas, that the public relations people will have prepared a single standard release, for distribution to the trade press, the *Financial Times*, the *Durham Advertiser* and the *News of the World*, and that some of the recipients are going to be a little baffled by the technicalities. It is essential that the company representative himself shall have seen a copy of the handout before his interview, in order to be able to relate it to the journalist who is coming to see him, so that this basic document can be made either simpler or more technical, according to the man and the paper involved. Many public relations departments inexplicably fail to do this, so that the unfortunate technical director, managing director or whoever he may be has to cope with a reporter's questions without knowing exactly what his own company has said.

It is worth bearing in mind, while being interviewed for a paper, that the information may not end up only with that particular paper. Many local reporters supply items to national papers as well, and to the news departments of the BBC and IBA, which may in turn send them overseas. An interview given on one's home ground for what one innocently imagined to be a purely local public may become a pebble thrown into a pond, with the ripples spreading further and further outwards. There is nothing one can do about it, nor does it particularly matter. However seriously one may have been misunderstood or misrepresented, any attempt to get a public apology or a correction inserted is rarely worth the trouble. It is as foolish and useless as a jilted woman's breach of promise action, which does no more than seek revenge for wounded pride and makes few friends in the process. A much more fruitful approach is to write to the editor, stressing that the letter is private, and saying, in effect, that mistakes happen everywhere, but that this particular one ought to be corrected in his files, in case the error perpetuates itself. An invitation to lunch, sent in the same letter, is a very sound plan. It makes a friend rather than an enemy and provides an opportunity to give the editor some useful background information about the company and the people who work for it.

Editors, unfortunately, are almost the only people on newspapers, other than very privileged correspondents, columnists and feature-writers, who are able to put appointments in their diary with any confidence. Reporters, who benefit enormously from leisurely conversations of this kind, rarely have them, simply because they are never sure what they are going to be doing on the following day. On the whole, the firms and Government departments who get the best treatment from the media are those who make a point of entertaining editors and correspondents regularly and when things are going normally and well, instead of waiting until some misfortune has occurred and then calling a press conference in order to explain and defend oneself.

One often overlooked link with the media usually receives far too little attention. This is the portrait archive in which photographs of the most newsworthy members of the staff are kept. It is very important that no photograph in this file should be more than two years old, and, a month or two before the two year life of the picture is up, a new one should be taken as a matter of routine and the old one added to the historical section. If this is not done, the man who appears in the newspapers and the man the public sees on television can exhibit the most obvious and humiliating differences. A particularly absurd example of this occurred in 1974, when the person involved was the extremely dictatorial and vain Chairman of one of Britain's top twenty companies. Despite frequent pleas from the Managing Director and the Public Relations Department, he insisted that the only photograph of him that was to be issued or reproduced for any purpose was one taken twenty-two years ago, since when over-good living had brought about certain sensational changes in his face. The phenomenon is not unknown outside Britain. It would have taken a skilled detective to have identified the fleshy and coarse-looking 1974 man from photographs of the slim and handsome 1952 man, and catastrophe occurred when, in the same television programme, the real man was interviewed in the studio and his former self appeared in a brief historical introduction to the achievements of the company. After that, the official portrait was quietly and irrevocably withdrawn and something more easily recognisable substituted.

Nowadays, televison producers much prefer colour slides

to the glossy prints which served as caption-stills for so many years. Slides give a more satisfactory colour range and they are easier to show. Few firms as yet have adjusted their routine to meet these new requirements and when asked for 'a picture of your Chairman' continue to supply the black and white prints, which are what the papers want. To be able to provide a slide creates an excellent impression.

Sir Michael Swann, the Chairman of the BBC's Board of Governors, recently gave it as his opinion,[1] that industrialists, as a category, were not very good on television. They gave, he believed, far too little attention to the art of putting over their case, they were too reticent, they allowed interviewers to make rings round them. Trade Union leaders, he thought, were much better at the job. The implication was that something ought to be done to improve the situation. In the remainder of this chapter we outline some of the ways in which this can be done, including radio in our field of action.

Radio, contrary to most people's belief, is a more difficult medium than television. It demands a higher standard of speaking, more quick-wittedness and, that great rarity, a voice which reflects the whole person. Good radio performers are less common than good television performers, but, on the other hand, some people to whom television is unkind do very well on radio. A game worth practising is to play a video-tape with the picture turned off and to ask a group of people to write down, in as much detail as possible, what they think the speaker looks like. The results are, for the most part, hilariously wrong, as is all too clear when the full face-and-voice recording is replayed. There are many variants of this game. One can ask the group, for example, to guess the age, the occupation, the kind of clothes that are being worn, the most frequent expression on the face, and so on, with only the voice to go by. Or one can carry out the exercise the other way round, fitting a voice one cannot hear to a face one can see. The results are always illuminating and tell the group a great deal about prejudices and stereotypes. If, for instance, one knows that the speaker on the sound-only tape is connected with industry or trade, most people expect him to look stern, determined, cleft-chinned and with a short-back-and-sides haircut, whereas in reality he is quite likely to be a cheerful, smiling extrovert or to have a quiet, reflective face which in no way fits into the no-doubts, decision-taking stereotype of the business executive.

That there is such a stereotype nobody can doubt and many businessmen make themselves anxious and miserable in their efforts to approximate to it. There is nothing new about such a situation. A visit to the refurbished Long Gallery at Montacute House in Somerset, which is now lined with Elizabethan and Jacobean portraits lent by the National Portrait Gallery is a somewhat alarming experience. All these successful lawyers, merchants and politicians have the same unsmiling, watch-out expression on their faces – 'grave' was the contemporary term. One passes the picture of one ruthless social pirate after another, men whose faces reflect their single-minded concentration on getting and keeping money and power. This was the stereotype, and no Elizabethan business-man would have accepted and paid for his portrait if the painter had failed to show him looking suitably 'grave'. In the same way, the fashionable American business face has changed three times during the past 120 years, from lean and tired-looking before the Civil War – the Abraham Lincoln face – to hard, smoother and much crueller during the years following the Civil War and up to 1914 – the Robber Baron face – and then to the always-smiling, rimless-glasses, milk-fed veal face of the 1920s–1960s. It now seems to be changing again, to something rather squarer, longer and less podgy, but it will probably be another five or ten years before the new stereo-type is fully formed.

The public is greatly influenced by stereotypes. It knows how people in different occupations should look and it feels frustrated and disappointed if the wrong kind of face comes up on the television screen. All butchers should be fat and have red faces, all generals should look slightly alcoholic and have the appropriate type of moustache, all policemen should

look and behave like the characters of *Z Cars* and *Softly,
Softly*, all clergymen should look saintly and slightly simple
and sport the famous clerical voice, all Trade Union leaders
should have a cloth-cap appearance. Men who really do look
like the stereotype start with enormous advantages; they are
accepted straight away for what they are, without any preliminary period of adjustment. Those who are unfortunate
enough merely to resemble themselves compel an audience
to waste precious time and energy, first wondering if they
have been confronted with an imposter and then gradually
getting used to the idea of a new-style policeman, Head of the
National Coal Board or whatever. People like the former
Archbishop of Canterbury, Dr Ramsey; the former General
Secretary of the Trades Union Congress, Lord Feather; the
Poet Laureate, Sir John Betjeman; and the Director-General
of the Confederation of British Industry, Sir Campbell Adam-
son, are exceedingly obliging in this respect: they look exactly
as the public expects people in their particular job to look and
sound. They are the stereotype made flesh.

Businessmen are no different from any other class of people.
They want to conform and to be well thought of by their
fellows and by the public. They know, or think they know,
what the correct stereotype is and most of them get as close
to it as they can. They wear what their observation tells them
to be appropriate clothes, hats and spectacle frames, they pay
careful attention to the length and shape of the various patches
of hair on their heads and, so far as they can, they cultivate
what they imagine to be the proper expression on their faces.
Television certainly increases the pressure to conform, mainly because conformity is a circular process. *Softly, Softly*
policemen look and talk as they do because the researchers,
scriptwriters and producers have spent a lot of time watching
and listening to real policemen, and real policemen become
super-real by watching and admiring the characters in *Softly,
Softly*. Doctors do the same, although many of them would
hotly deny it, and so do politicians.

There are two ways of looking at this. One can say that a

stable society needs stock types, in order to keep its social bearings. The stock types are permitted to change gently and gradually, provided not all of them change at once, but anything drastic and sudden is disturbing and, by most people, unwanted. This was well shown after the Revolution in Russia and after the collapse of the Nazi regime in Germany in 1945. All the old stereotypes had to be thrown overboard and forgotten and a new set created, for use in books, newspapers, magazines, films, radio and on the stage. The stereotype revolution was as profound and far-reaching as the political revolution and inseparable from it. For a long time people did not know where they were; the devils and angels had changed places and there was a whole new series of characters whom one had to learn to recognise as good or bad, with unpleasant consequences if one failed to get it right. Something very similar went on in all the Central European countries and in many parts of Africa during the 1950s and 1960s and it has since become noticeable in a number of Asian countries. The process is particularly difficult and painful for middle-aged and elderly people, whose stereotypes, like their arteries, have progressively hardened over the years.

People like, then, to know where they are and stereotypes are a way of giving them a few fixed points around which their lives can revolve. But, on the other hand, stereotypes can be and often are a very serious brake on progress and change. They can encourage prejudices which are no longer well founded and make it very difficult for original and creative minds to flourish as they should. In certain cases they are, to put the point bluntly, a thorough nuisance. Both business and politics have undoubtedly suffered unnecessarily and a great deal from out-of-date stereotypes. In Britain the industrial image is bad and it is not easy, even today, when jobs are hard to find, to persuade intelligent and well-educated young men and women to go into anything connected with manufacturing, buying or selling. This must obviously have something to do with the businessman as the media present him, and it is worth asking exactly what picture of him comes across, and how this conflicts with the way in which British business is actually carried on and with the real people who earn a living by running it.

A useful question to ask any businessman is, 'what job do you expect you'll be doing after the Communist takeover in Britain?' After recovering from the initial shock of this rather direct approach, a high proportion answer, either in effect or in these very words, 'Oh, I'm not worried. I'm a professional manager, and Communism needs professional managers just as much as capitalism does.' This is perfectly true in general terms, but the fact remains that Communism needs some kinds of professional managers much more than others. It has, for example, no need whatever for the professional managers employed by property companies and very little for those working in insurance. The core of the statement is, however, correct. Trained, skilled, experienced managers are likely to be in demand, no matter what the political shape of any particular society may be, and the great majority of what we call businessmen are no more or less than employed, professional managers, who do much the same kind of work, whether their employer happens to be ICI, the Post Office, the Coal Board, British Leyland or the National Westminster Bank.

There are two wretchedly unfortunate words which completely confuse and debase the image of the modern businessman, that is, of the professional manager. One is 'industry' and the other 'industrialist'. The problem is of recent origin, and has arisen mainly from the need to find a comprehensive word to include in the name of the national employers' association, the Confederation of British Industry. The Confederation of British Manufacturers would not do, because the CBI represents, or claims to represent, organisations concerned with transport and various kinds of services, as well as with manufacturing, all of which are nowadays called industries. Since farmers also speak of 'the agricultural industry', there seems to be no reason why agriculture, too, should not come under the CBI, and one day, perhaps, it will do so. But what, it may be asked, is wrong with the words 'industry' and 'industrialist'? Why is their influence so malignant?

The answer is, alas, that they are much too grand and pompous and that they suggest, especially to the younger generation, the bad old world of private ownership, large profits and exploited workers. Difficult as it may be for the CBI and for certain sections of the Conservative Party to realise this, 'industry' and 'industrialist' are not neutral, technical terms. They are, under present circumstances, socially divisive and every hard-working manager who goes into a British television studio labelled 'industrialist' is in difficulties from the start. The industrialist-stereotype contains these ingredients:

a. Overweight, from a life of luxurious eating and drinking and very little exercise.

b. Rich, probably indecently rich, with a shareholding of at least hundreds of thousands in his company.

c. Rolls-Royce, clubs, port, cigars, Caribbean holidays, cruises, mansions, race-horses.

d. Coarse-fibred, semi-educated at best, living only for money-making.

e. Anti-union.

f. Loud-voiced, aggressive, bad-tempered.

g. Very far to the political right.

It is, in fact, the portrait of the capitalist as the world Communist press sees him. The fact that most of the people who occupy high industrial posts are not like this at all does little, as yet, to modify the stereotype. There are still sufficient industrial and commercial grandees around, both in Europe and America, with all the characteristics summarised under *a–g* above, to perpetuate the image. For progressive, efficient, liberal-minded managers it is a grievous handicap, from which one day they will have to rid themselves. As things stand now, however, this is the image which television encourages, aided and abetted by the newspaper gossip columnists, who would go out of business without a good supply of

vulgar and despicable business tycoons and their even more
vulgar and despicable women.

   To say that television encourages the public to continue to
think about businessmen in the old terms calls for an explanation. How and why does it do this? The first reason has already
been given: because the public loves stereotypes and needs
them like a drug, and the business of the mass media is to give
the public what it wants. The second reason is slightly more
complicated. The editors and producers of television interviews and discussions like their characters to have sharp,
easily defined edges. Barmaids should be blonde and busty,
military men should bark and have small moustaches, footballers should be unmistakably footballers and dukes dukes.
This makes it much easier to cast, arrange and direct the
entertainment, which is all a television item really is. If it is
fixing up one of its notoriously unhelpful and uncreative both-
sides-of-industry discussions, it does its best to get a trade
unionist who looks and sounds like everybody's idea of a trade
unionist, and 'an industrialist' who performs a similar service
for his side of the fence. The fact that both are likely to be
caricatures helps the producer and helps the viewer, in the
sense that battle is joined between two recognisably different
species of animal. Nobody but a spoil-sport or a purist is likely
to object. The public, one is always told, likes it that way.

   There are, in fact, two sides of industry, but not altogether
in the way television folklore suggests. Physically, management and the shop floor are different, at least in Britain. Whatever the anti-racialists and the egalitarians may say to the
contrary, there is a managerial head and a managerial way of
carrying it on the shoulders. This is not to go quite as far as to
say that one can recognise an English Roman Catholic by his
walk, a claim once made to the present writer by the Borough
Librarian of a town in Somerset. The fact remains, however,
that if one has spent one's working life giving orders rather
than taking them, in the security of a salary and professional
qualifications rather than in insecurity of a weekly wage and
no paper qualifications at all, in a collar and tie and a good suit,

rather than in grubby open-necked shirt and overalls, then these differences show in the expression on one's face, in one's bearing and even in the features, which tend to be noticeably more refined among those doing clean, very responsible work than among those carrying out heavy or unskilled manual tasks. There is, in short, a kind of face which is common enough among both men and women on the managerial level, but which is very rarely found on the shop floor, as any un-biassed walk around a range of factories will show. If one's father and grandfather also lived comfortable lives and were command-givers, rather than command-takers, the differ-ences are likely to be even more marked than they are in the case of a first-generation manager.

It is not entirely true that one can do nothing about this and that one simply has to accept that there are significant physical differences between managers and the managed, rulers and the ruled. One can be superior, to use an old-fashioned but still useful word, in one's appearance and modest and friendly in one's dress or behaviour, or one can look superior and behave arrogantly. To indicate observable physical differences is not in the least to support the idea of a master-race, nor to suggest that these ideas are necessarily permanent. One can envisage and hope for a form of society in which brutalising, demoralising, idiotic work has been eliminated and it would be very surprising if that failed to reflect itself in the faces of the population.

There are certain important things to consider, apart from one's face, when one is deciding whether or not to accept an invitation to appear on a television or radio programme. These can be summarised in the form of questions to oneself.

1. Why do they want me? Would someone else do as well, or better?

2. Who needs whom most? On this particular occasion, do I need the BBC more than they need me, or is it the other way round?

3. What is likely to happen if I refuse?
4. What complications do I foresee (a) if I accept, (b) if I refuse?
5. Is this something I am likely to enjoy, or should I simply accept the role of a sacrificial figure and get on with it?

The broadcasting people themselves, of course, will never see the matter in these terms. So far as they are concerned, it is always a privilege to appear in one of their programmes, and a refusal is incomprehensible. The prospective performer, however, is entitled to look after his own interests and to engage in ground-clearing operations before he says yes or no. It is safe to reckon that the media are most likely to show an interest in the affairs of oneself or one's company when something has gone wrong – a strike, redundancies, an explosion, a shut-down, a boardroom row – and that industry at peace, like anything else in a state of quiet efficiency, rarely calls for attention. Where business is concerned, telephone calls from the media are bound to be ominous and hardly to meet with a joyful reception. There are, of course, exceptions to this. Positive achievements are, fortunately, newsworthy from time to time and one should never give up hope.

Editors and producers always like to have the top man if they can get him, and if he is not known to be unco-operative or an impossibly bad performer. This is not only a matter of prestige. The more responsible post someone occupies, the more likely he is to be in possession of all the relevant facts and to be able to answer questions with authority. 'The top man' does not always mean the very top man. It can, and often does, mean the head of a division or department, if this should happen to be the person with the greatest amount of relevant knowledge of the subject under discussion. Some managing directors, regional controllers and directors-general are always in and out of broadcasting studios. They enjoy the experience and they would hate to see what they regard as a privilege and opportunity taken away from them and given to any of their colleagues. Others have never been known to appear and are only too pleased to hand over the thankless task to someone else.

But whether the company spokesman goes willingly or unwillingly, he should make it his business to speak personally on the telephone to the producer, editor, presenter or reporter who has made the approach. This is not a job to be left to a personal assistant or a secretary, for the very good reason that it is not the personal assistant or secretary who eventually has to appear in the studio. A telephone conversation is a first rehearsal, and should be treated as such. 'What,' the producer should be asked, 'is the story at present, as you see it?' If it turns out that the producer has been seriously misinformed, he should be told so, and at that point what was originally a story may well develop into a non-story and die there and then. If, on the other hand, there is a story, the producer should be asked what line he proposes to follow, whether any supporting film is to be used and, if so, what will it show, and whether any other people are to appear in the same item? All these are perfectly reasonable questions, and an indication that the two parties are meeting on a basis of equality, not of master and servant.

Never, unless one is passionately fond of driving, accept an invitation which will involve one in an exhausting journey before the programme. A 50-mile drive in January across icy or foggy roads is hardly calculated to deliver a speaker at the studio in prime condition, a fact which producers frequently tend to overlook. One should draw attention to this and, if no company car and driver is available, insist that the BBC or IBA provides one, and, if necessary, agrees to pay for overnight accommodation. This, incidentally, is a good way of discovering an answer to the question, 'who needs whom most?' Producers, with their budgets to consider, will naturally resist requests for transport, but, if they are really determined to obtain a particular speaker, they will provide it.

If one does eventually decide to take part in a programme, it is important not to take the matter too seriously. Broadcasting, whether by television or by radio, is a medium with a never-satisfied appetite for facts and entertainment. Nothing is remembered for long and one's golden words disappear on the breeze almost as soon as one has spoken them. The best performers realise this and have come to terms with it. They provide a few minutes of what they hope is agreeable conversation in an untidy room which resembles a workshop much more than a theatre, and depart. If they have been invited because they are known to be experts on the matter under discussion, they have the immense comfort of knowing that they almost certainly know a great deal more about the subject than the interviewer or any of the listeners or viewers. There is no point in worrying about information one forgot to give or points one failed to make. The only person who is aware of this is the expert himself.

Never take any notes into the studio – there will be no opportunity to use them – and never make the slightest attempt to write anything out in advance or to memorise anything more than one or two basic facts. In broadcasting one has to paint with a very broad brush and to remember that the medium is a very unsatisfactory way of communicating information. Statistics are never understood and one should attempt nothing more ambitious than, 'We've made £14 million more profit this year than last', or, 'We're being forced to get rid of 200 men'. On television, it is not what one says that is important, but, from the point of view of the audience, whether one gives the impression of being a pleasant, honest person and, from the point of view of the producer, whether one responds energetically to questions and stops when one is told to stop. 'A good company spokesman' means much the same as 'a good broadcaster' or, to use a dreadful but much used phrase, 'a good television personality' – a likeable, trustworthy person with a flavour to him.

No-one who has broadcasting ambitions should be deprived of the experience of asking a group of people, chosen more or less at random, to write down what they think are the main points one has just made in the course of an interview. The results of such an exercise are usually better for radio than for television, where there is more to distract the attention of an audience away from one's words, but they will almost invariably reveal that to attempt to put across one or two main points in the course of three or four minutes is a complete waste of time. Very skilled performers will, nevertheless, be aware of the kind of phrase or opinion which is likely to get reported in the newspapers, and will take good care to provide a reasonable ration of these, irrespective of whether they have much direct relevance to the discussion.

One should always ask, when making a broadcasting appearance, 'How can I get the maximum advantage for myself out of this?' not 'Am I doing what the BBC expected me to do?' The BBC has ways of looking after itself, but broadcasting is essentially and all the time a battle of wits and the slow-witted are not likely to survive and prosper. This does not mean – and it is impossible to make the point too often or too strongly – jumping in to talk almost before the interviewer has finished his question. It is extremely effective to delay beginning one's reply for a few seconds, so that viewers can look at one's face and wonder what one is going to say. A pause of this kind heightens interest and provides a useful opportunity for gathering one's thoughts. One can do this on television, even for as long as four or five seconds, but not on radio, which makes television the easier medium.

As anyone who has been in a television control gallery will know, the programme director has several screens – monitors – in front of him, showing the pictures which are available to him at any given moment. In an interview or discussion he can cut from this to that face as he pleases or show more than one person at a time. His choice is not confined, of course, to the person who happens to be speaking. If someone else on the programme – it may be the honoured guest while the interviewer is putting his question – should happen to yawn, scratch his ear, look bored or perplexed or gaze up to Heaven for help, one can be almost certain that the director will cut away from the speaker in order to catch this shot. Experienced performers are well aware of this possibility and can score off an opponent without saying a word, in the knowledge that viewers will see them silently covering their eyes, wrinkling their nose or pursing their lips as an indication of their feelings.

Nobody can put on a decent performance if he is physically uncomfortable and one should ask for one's seating position to be adjusted until one can be reasonably sure of avoiding intolerable cramp and of seeing the interviewer properly without the need of turning one's head through 90 degrees. The lighting man and the sound man may object, but there is no need whatever to pay any attention to their feelings. They are there to help the producer get the best results, not to make life easy for themselves. Disregard also any instructions to 'use more voice', that is, to speak more loudly. The business of the director and the technicians is to take people as they are. Microphone positions and amplifier settings can be changed to turn a semi-whisper into a shout and nothing and nobody should persuade a speaker to talk at any other than his or her normal conversational level.

Within limits, one can wear what one likes when appearing on television and it is rare to be given any advice or instructions in the matter. One or two basic points are worth noting, however. White clothes, which, in the case of men, usually means white shirts, are to be avoided. They dazzle the camera, and by forcing it to half-close its lens in self-defence, cause the face to receive less attention than it should. A white-shirted person is, unavoidably, a dark or even black-faced person and few of us find this flattering. Very dark clothes are equally unsuitable. They result in over-exposure of the lighter areas, which include the face and neck, and in undesirable effects of a different nature. Large, bold checks cause problems with scanning, but small checks and any vigorous patterning which is not rectangular or striped are perfectly in order. Nothing should be worn which is likely to puzzle viewers or demand too much of their attention. This means that one should leave club or regimental ties behind in the wardrobe – they may be recognisable in colour but they do nothing but baffle the person who is forced to look at them in black and white. Badges, too, should be forgotten, unless there is any plan to use them as a visual aid during the performance.

There is some disagreement about the wisdom of taking alcohol before appearing on television, a not infrequent habit among men from the business world. All one can say with certainty is that with some skins, mostly of the opaque or vellum type, alcohol in the blood-stream is very likely to produce blotches on the face and hands. These are, for some reason, much more noticeable on television than on a face-to-face occasion. One can do no more than experiment to discover one's personal reactions, but few people would disagree that such alcoholic blotches do neither oneself nor one's employers a great deal of credit.

There is considerable art in the positioning of speakers for a television discussion and some people are affronted by being put out on the wings of the group, rather than in the centre or by the side of the chairman, seats to which they feel their importance entitles them. In general, the principle is to put speakers who are known to be aggressive, over-talkative and inclined to monopolise the proceedings at either end of the group, rather than in the middle and, conversely, to bring less confident people to the central position. This helps to discipline and tame those who need such treatment and to give courage and a feeling of being wanted to the timid ones. What the producer wants above everything else is something as close to a fight as he can decently get, and he will place his group in what seems to him the pattern most calculated to achieve this. He will not object to the occasional burst of anger, real or contrived, nor to a certain amount of tumult, with one person talking or shouting over another, but it is well, for the sake of one's own reputation, not to overdo either of these. The bad-tempered businessman is not a very appealing figure and unless one is grossly provoked it is best to leave this sort of thing to the politicians, to whom it comes as naturally and fittingly as bogus grimaces of pain to all-in wrestlers.

A television programme can find its way to its audience by means of a live transmission, a recording or film, and there are advantages and disadvantages in all three. From the performer's point of view, the live studio transmission is probably the safest, since he has the comfort of knowing that his words will go out exactly as he said them and in their entirety. He may not be very satisfied with the result, and he may feel that a second version would have been better, either as a whole or in part, but, good or bad, nobody will have had a chance to edit his remarks. Editing is possible with a tele-recording, made from a studio performance, but this is unlikely to happen with a regional programme, mainly on the grounds of expense. A repeat recording is sometimes made, but not very often, since, to the great surprise of many people, a second take is usually not as good as the first and, in any case, it has to be paid for.

A studio performance, either live or recorded, is cheaper than film. There is no processing, no editing, no cost of getting the film crew to the location. On the other hand, film does allow considerable tidying up and compression, and it provides atmosphere and background in a way that is not possible in the studio. Many a long-winded, woolly-minded speaker has reason to be grateful to a film editor for removing great slabs of sheer verbosity from his replies, a kindness which is performed equally efficiently and equally often by the editors of sound tapes for radio. Important public figures not infrequently demand either to be present when film is edited or to be shown the results, for their approval or disapproval, before the film is transmitted. This is almost impossible and the broadcasting companies do well to stand out against it. Editing is a highly professional job, and it has to be done at great speed, at least for the news or magazine programmes for which these filmed items are almost invariably destined. If performers were given the right to censor the cut versions of their films, the broadcasting machine would grind to a halt.

One is therefore obliged to trust the producer. He will almost invariably use only a small part of what was filmed, but, whatever the general opinion may be, it is very uncommon to find one's meaning wilfully or ignorantly distorted. If one is afraid that one's contribution will be massacred, the surest form of defence is to be brief and to the point and to avoid all preliminaries and lengthy conclusions. In this way, there will be far less to cut. Apart from this, there is a very simple way of keeping a check on what happens after the film unit has departed from one's office, factory, farm, home or wherever the work has been carried out. Always have a small battery-driven tape-recorder to hand on these occasions. Place it out of shot on the ground and set it going before the interview begins. One then has a complete record of the interview, and of any parts of it which may be repeated, and, should there be any reason to complain of subsequent distortion, the original version is there as evidence.

One caution is very necessary to busy men. Never believe an editor or reporter when he says over the telephone that the whole filming job can be over and done within an hour. Always allow at least two hours. Equipment has a habit of breaking down and needing to be put right, aeroplanes, banging doors, compressors and other extraneous noises cause retake after retake, the reporter realises half way through that the story needs to be angled in a slightly different way, and two hours speed by with no difficulty at all. Remember, too, that the film unit may have come a long way and quite possibly got up very early in order to arrive on time. Always offer them some refreshment before they start work and again before they leave. The public relations value of this is enormous and the cheerful atmosphere it engenders can speed up the proceeding considerably.

A final piece of advice is one which one would prefer not to have to give, but experience proves it, alas, to be very necessary. Do not, however important you may be in your own field, expect privileged or red carpet treatment at a television studio or on a filming occasion. Even if it could be provided, it would undermine the essentially democratic nature of the proceedings, produce a worse programme and deprive the Great Man of a valuable experience. Television producers do not think in the hierarchical terms which are normal to businessmen.

With the whole human panorama passing before them every day, they do not see people as great men, less great men and men who are not great at all. Their perspective shows them only nice people and nasty people, helpful people and obstructive people, intelligent people and fools. It does no harm, however eminent one may be, to be regarded, after one has done one's stint and left the building, as one of the nice people.

REFERENCE

1. *The Times*, July 2, 1975.

7. *Reasonable and unreasonable demands made by employers*

This chapter is really an attempt to discover a workable definition of loyalty. It is probably the most difficult problem that has to be faced when one appears in public as a spokesman for one's employers, and, like the hardly less important matters of basic education and personal culture, it is usually totally ignored in courses which aim at improving one's ability as a speaker. The present writer does not believe, and in previous chapters has said so as plainly as he can, that technique is everything and that there is anything to be proud of in being able to create the illusion that one is saying something, when in fact one is saying nothing. This seems to him to be a thoroughly immoral and pernicious attitude, as dangerous and as stupid as saying that one can learn to write well, even if one has nothing to write about. In nine cases out of ten, if a man or woman is poor at communication, and communication, it should be remembered, involves communicating attitudes and emotions, as well as facts, the cause is either fear – one does not feel free to tell the audience what one knows it should be told – or ignorance – one's experience has been too limited, one's circle of friends and acquaintances too narrow, one's stock of information too small, one's touch and taste unsure. No amount of 'practical instruction' can make up for these fundamental deficiencies, but plenty of businessmen go on courses, often expensive courses, under the impression that, given a teacher who knows his business, a sow's ear can be transformed into a silk purse in a few weeks, or even days.

What, for instance, is a prospective student likely to infer from syllabuses, drawn up by highly reputable institutions, which tickle his palate with phrases like:

> A series of short intensive courses at high level intended for men and women in positions of responsibility in business and the professions. The courses are wholly practical and designed to give members self-confidence, efficiency, authority and distinction in spoken communication, both formal and informal.[1]

or:

> At the end of two days' tuition, practice and constructive critical appraisal, participants should have made considerable improvements in their techniques of addressing the group.[2]

Busy people are naturally attracted by the thought that they are enrolling for something that is 'practical', since they like to think of themselves as 'practical' people, but it is frankly dishonest to suggest that anyone can be given 'self-confidence, efficiency, authority and distinction in spoken communication' in a short course, however 'intensive' and however experienced and hard-working the tutor may be. It is possible to make a person a little more self-confident in a couple of days and to show him how to set about the task of organising and presenting his material in a more satisfactory way, which is presumably what is meant by 'efficiency'. What certainly cannot be done is to add 'authority' and 'distinction' to the performance of men and women who lack these qualities. 'Authority' and 'distinction' are not an impressive veneer, glued on by a skilled craftsman, they come from within a person and they take many years to develop, if they ever develop at all.

A so-called practical course is easy, because it avoids all the complications, disappointments and new starts which anything worthy of the name education must inevitably involve. One can teach the techniques of carpentry or dressmaking relatively quickly to people who may quite well spend the rest of their lives using these techniques to make ill-designed, hideous, vulgar objects. The cultivation of taste and discrimination and a sense of good design, on the other hand, takes a long time and requires very favourable circumstances. Without these fundamental qualities, however, mere technique, however brilliant, is worthless. The value of a short course is not that it is self-contained – it can never be that – but that it provides an opportunity to show the people who attend it what the problems are and how to go away and overcome them. And most of these problems are philosophical, not technical, however inconvenient and administratively untidy a fact this might be.

Loyalty to one's employer is a philosophical problem, not a technical problem, and to discuss it fruitfully and creatively necessitates breaking certain taboos, which we shall now proceed to do. There are, as the late David Lloyd George once pointed out, three kinds of loyalty. One can be loyal to an institution, to a person, or to an idea. He himself, he had come to realise, had practically no sense of loyalty to institutions, some to persons, or at any rate to selected persons, and a great deal to ideas. This, naturally, made him an object of great suspicion to those who gave a very high priority to loyalty to institutions, such as a school, a university, a club, the House of Commons, a regiment, the Monarchy or the British Empire. But, as he often pointed out, he had never been to what the British call a public and the Americans, more logically, a private school, or to a college or university, or spent several years in one of the services. His institutional bump was not well developed, and he had not been able to make up his mind as to whether the Monarchy or the Empire were institutions or ideas.

A firm, like a school or a Civil Service department or the police force, is an institution, and one of the main reasons why so many old-established firms have preferred to recruit ex-public school boys – public school girls are quite another matter – to their staff is that, with rare and unfortunate exceptions, public school boys have been trained for many years to place a very high value on loyalty to institutions. They can be, from this point of view, 'depended on'.

But what, in fact, does loyalty to the institution mean? It means, broadly speaking, standing up for it through thick and thin in front of people who do not themselves belong to it, to the outside world. It means my company, my department, my school, my regiment, right or wrong. Now, in certain circumstances, this may be a very necessary and commendable attitude. The head of any concern must, if he is to deserve any respect at all, defend members of his staff against attacks from outside. The public sacrifice of individuals to mob criticism is not a pretty sight and weakens morale among the colleagues of the victims. In private, anything may happen and often does, but in public the united front is the only defensible policy. Where the united front is allowed, and even encouraged, to become a disunited front, as happened in the case of the British Cabinet during the weeks preceding the referendum on Britain's membership of the European Economic Community, the result is disastrous. The Cabinet is rightly expected to be of one mind, and so is the Foreign Office, the Department of the Environment or any other official body.

The same principle cannot, however, be applied to the Cabinet, or for that matter, Parliament as institutions. It would be nonsense to suggest that the composition of the Cabinet is ideal for all time, or that Parliament should never be reformed in any detail, and totally irresponsible to bar all Ministers or Members from discussing such ideas or from putting forward strong or controversial opinions on the subject. No institution, even one as long established as the British Parliament, benefits from enforced fossilisation and senility.

Many business firms have come to regard themselves as being indistinguishable from the Cabinet, or perhaps one should say from the Cabinet as it was before 1975. They expect their staff, on all public occasions, not only to paper over all internal differences of opinion, which is not unreasonable, but to pretend that the firm never makes mistakes, an attitude which is patently absurd and which can put anyone who speaks under its banner in an impossible position. The problem then is where to draw the line. How much should the public be permitted to know?

As a rough guide, anybody who is given the probably unenviable task of representing his employers to the outside world, whether that world is a Rotary lunch or *Panorama*, should be given the freedom to admit that the organisation he works for is 90 per cent excellent and 10 per cent fallible, human and stupid. This corresponds fairly closely to the truth, in the case of a really first-class firm. For plenty of others, the ratio would be more like 50 per cent excellent and 50 per cent lamentable, but no harm whatever is done, for this particular purpose, by pretending that very mediocre firms are equal to the best. To admit 10 per cent fallibility is to give a spokesman room to manoeuvre; to deny it to him is to make him cruelly vulnerable. No organisation, not even Marks and Spencer, can possibly be flawless and to work for something which is 90 per cent first-class is to be very fortunate indeed. Only extreme vanity or extreme fear – 'Once we open the floodgates', etc. – could produce the 'we are 100 per cent marvellous' stance, and only extreme sadism could force one's employees to present such a ridiculous view in public.

Once the 10 per cent-not-perfect possibility is accepted, the whole situation changes and the speaker can breathe. Let us consider one or two actual situations in order to see how this new-found freedom would work out in practice. We might select as our organisations-in-shackles, the Amalgamated Union of Building Trades Workers, the National Union of Teachers, the Post Office, British Rail, British Airways and English China Clays, all of them bodies which are nationally and locally frequently on stage.

To the Amalgamated Union of Building Trades Workers, the National Union of Teachers, and any other trade union body, all members are, beyond argument or denial, equal and paragons. They are equally skilled, equally hard working, equally public-spirited, equalling self-sacrificing and equally patriotic. The difficulty is that the public knows otherwise and, as a result, spokesmen for this or any other union, may have to find ways of closing a rather wide and obvious credibility gap in order to get their case accepted. An excellent, and from the Union's point of view, exceedingly embarrassing instance of this occurred when certain of its members were convicted of manifestly unpeaceful picketing during a strike. To put the matter more plainly, they were found guilty of thuggish, violent intimidation of their fellow workers and they were quite rightly sent to prison, where they somewhat surprisingly achieved not infamy and disgrace, but martyrdom, being sanctified first as the Shrewsbury Seven and then, as they were, like the Ten Little Nigger Boys, released one by one, as the Shrewsbury Six, the Shrewsbury Five and so on, until there was one.

It would have been a simple matter for the Union to have said at the outset, 'These are our black sheep. They fully deserve what they've got and we completely dissociate ourselves from them as a union. The great bulk of our members are quiet, law-abiding, decent men, not like the Shrewsbury Seven in the least. We wholly approve of the Court's decision, and we shall do everything in our power to make sure that beastliness of this kind doesn't happen in the future.'

This would have been to follow the 90:10 principle. It would have been truthful, intelligible and very good for brightening up the Union's somewhat tarnished image. The whole incident could then have been buried and forgotten. But, most unfortunately, the Union decided to tell the world on every possible occasion that all its members, without exception, were shining angels and that for this reason the Shrewsbury Seven were innocent and blameless beyond all question. This idiotic and unstatesmanlike stand may have satisfied the militant left, but it piled up a great deal of subsequent trouble, both for the Union and the TUC, who found themselves compelled over and over again to defend the indefensible, which committed them to talking nonsense, to clashing with the Home Secretary and to appearing ridiculous and contemptible in the eyes of the public, a result which can hardly have been in the minds of the Union Executive when it decided to take the coward's way out, the 'we are 100 per cent perfect' way out. 'We are 90 per cent perfect' demands a great deal more courage, but it is far less likely to lead to trouble in the long run.

The National Union of Teachers has not, to date, had to deal with the public relations problem of having a group of its more violent militants in prison, but in other ways its policy and its consequent difficulties are not dissimilar to those of the Amalgamated Union of Building Trades Workers. It operates from the same basic assumption, which even the briefest acquaintance with members of the teaching profession might cause one to think might be a little exaggerated, that all teachers are highly intelligent, sparklingly up-to-date, devoted to their profession, grossly overworked and seriously underpaid. Any suggestion that some of them might just possibly be better than others, that one or two might be more interested in the money than the job or just ticking over while waiting for retirement and doing the minimum meanwhile, is certain to be branded as malicious and ill-informed. So too is the merest hint of a thought that quite a lot of teachers are totally unsuited to the job and would do everybody, themselves included, a good turn by looking for alternative employment.

The NUT tactics are the nowadays familiar ones of never attempting to reason with its critics in public, but of simply ridiculing them or shouting them down. 'Anyone who does not agree with every word we say is an ignorant reactionary, unworthy to have his views expressed or heard.' It is no use arguing that this is not the best way to make friends or to create a good public image for teachers, although both of these conclusions are correct. A modern union does not aim to persuade the public to agree with its policy and its actions. Persuasion is believed to be a completely outmoded way of getting what one wants; coercion and bullying are much more effective and much more rapid, or so it is believed. The result is that NUT spokesmen are utterly predictable, dull and unconvincing when one sees them on television. They have never learnt the art of giving an inch in order to gain a yard; it is, in any case, an art which they give every sign of despising. 'If only,' one yearns to say to them, 'you could bring yourselves to admit that even 1 per cent of teachers were played out, incompetent or lazy, how much readier we should be to accept all the other things you tell us. If you could see just a few disadvantages and immaturities in the comprehensive system and just a few merits in the grammar schools, how much more convincing your advocacy of a non-selective system might be. But, as it is, the people who speak in your name sound like Communist puppets on May Day, and leave us with the strong suspicion that the schools of Britain exist not so much in order to give children an opportunity to learn and to be taught as to give as many teachers as possible a chance to earn as large a salary as possible.'

Spokesmen for the Post Office and for British Rail sometimes make us wonder if the same might not possibly be true of these two large organisations as well. It is all very well for important executives in the Post Office to write more-in-sorrow-than-in-anger letters to *The Times*, saying that it would be impossible to find a better body of men to work with, at all levels, or for equally highly placed people at British Rail headquarters to say that everyone is doing his best under very difficult circumstances. Nobody is suggesting that the Post Office is staffed from top to bottom by a bunch of incompetent crooks or that British Rail is run by people who cannot even read and count. All that one is asking for is a simple admission, in concrete, meaningful language, that certain blunders and miscalculations have been made and that certain unnecessary burdens are being carried, and the whole case suddenly becomes more believable and attractive.

The ranks close and the blinds fall too completely and too often. Over the past few years, one has been waiting in vain for statements of this kind:

On behalf of the Post Office

1. 'We know it was idiotic to introduce the system of first and second class mail, but now we're saddled with it and we don't know how to get rid of it.'

2. 'We realise all too well now, when it's too late, that putting up postal and telephone charges simply reduces the demand and slashes our income. Yes, of course it's true that by cutting our rates, rather than increasing them we could have made people use our services a great deal more and have created a bigger profit for ourselves. But we've got a tired, demoralised, unimaginative top management and they really don't want to be bothered with all the problems and complications of expansion just before they retire. Much safer and easier to let things run down gently.'

3. 'A lot of our troubles with mail arise from the fact that we're forced to use the railways wherever we can. It would be much quicker, easier and cheaper for us to take everything by road and air, but the railways need our traffic as a subsidy, so that's that.'

4. 'Yes, of course, it would be more sensible to have only one delivery a day, rather than put up charges, but it would mean that we should need fewer men, and the Union would resist that to the death.'

5. 'You're absolutely right, it is a scandal to charge so much for installing a new telephone. It would be much more sensible to put it in for almost nothing and to get our money back by having a pricing-policy which persuaded people to use their telephone a lot once they've got it.'

British Rail/London Transport

1. 'Guards are completely unnecessary on the Underground and why we still hang on to them, I can't imagine. Sheer conservatism and union pressure. As a matter of fact, we're the only metro in the world to have guards now. We could save an awful lot of money by abolishing them.'

2. 'Yes, I know it's stupid to have barriers and ticket-checkers at main-line stations. Travelling ticket-checkers are much more convenient and much cheaper. But the Union would never allow us to get rid of the men at the barrier.'

3. 'Having a second man in the cab of a diesel locomotive makes no sense at all. We know that. He's got absolutely nothing to do. He's just a hang-over from the old steam-engine days, when the driver and the fireman both had a real job. All these completely useless men cost us millions a year. But the Unions won't let us phase them out.'

4. 'A time-keeping bonus for drivers simply isn't on, un-fortunately, much as we should love to introduce it. Yes, it's quite true that France and several other countries have got it. But conditions are different here, and, anyway, the Union wouldn't allow it.'

5. 'Three-quarters of our rolling stock is obsolete and at least a quarter of it's an absolute disgrace. We need a huge replacement programme and it ought to be started straight away. Certainly it would provide work for thousands of people, but the stumbling block's the Government. For some reason we don't understand – Labour votes in Birmingham and Coventry, I suppose – they prefer to pump millions into British Leyland, and if ever anything was money down the drain, that's it.'

If one could hear and see people talking like that, what a breath of fresh air it would be and how the public's attention and interest would come alive. Here, at last, one should say, is someone prepared to build on solid ground, on real situations. The public relations revolution would have taken place. Whitewashing would have ceased to be the supreme art, and genuine people, instead of automata, would be seen on our television screens and quoted in our newspapers. To say 'impossible' is to condemn us to the present situation of non-communication for ever, and that would be truly in-tolerable, both for society and for the unfortunate men who feel they are compelled to talk nonsense in the public interest.

There are those who believe that it is immaterial if someone holding a post of great responsibility produces words that nobody can understand. The important thing is that he is there on the platform or in front of the cameras and microphones at all. According to this view, it is his presence that matters, not what he says. For a very few people in the world this may be true. It would be interesting to have Solzhenitsyn or Mao Tse-tung about the place, even if they did no more than recite the alphabet. The Chairman of the Post Office, or the Imperial Tobacco Company, however, are not quite in the same class and they make a more satisfactory impact if they have something concrete and definite to say, which, unfortunately, they rarely do.

It is not that they deliberately set out to tell lies, but that long years spent trying to avoid trouble have brought them to a point at which it is second nature to refuse to commit oneself, to be, as they hope, pleasantly vague ('diplomatic') and to deny that one's own side could possibly be in error. With businessmen this is rarely quite as bad as with politicians, where it has become a very dangerous disease, which corrupts the speaker himself and destroys the possibility of anything one might call communication. It amounts to saying that the public cannot be trusted with truth and anyone who believes this and builds his life style around it will eventually find himself exposed for the sham he is.

One recalls, with despair, an occasion during the early summer of 1975 when the British Foreign Secretary, Mr Callaghan, was appearing on a BBC phone-in programme, *Referendum Call*. Mr Callaghan was known to be strongly in favour of Britain continuing to be a member of the EEC. He belonged, whether from conviction or from prudence, to the 'Yes' faction of the Goverment. A Mrs Levy asked him over the telephone link about the three leaflets which had been put through the letterbox of every household in the country, and she received this explanation from the Foreign Secretary:

You will have three pamphlets. One will be the Government's

recommendation to the British people to stay in; the second,
prepared by the pro-Marketeers, will say why you should
vote *Yes*; and the third will be by the anti-Marketeers saying
why you should vote *No*. I do recommend you to read all three,
but particularly, in view of the Government's recommendation, to read that one most importantly (sic).

That seemed clear enough to Mrs Levy, and she said, perfectly reasonably, 'Then there are two for and one against?'
Mr Callaghan then produced an historic masterpiece of non-
think, Newspeak. 'No,' he replied, 'there is one for and one
against, and there is the third one, which is the Government's
view, which comes down in favour, on balance, of Britain
remaining a member of the Community.'

Mr Robin Day, who was in the chair, felt it to be his duty
to knock a little sense into Mr Callaghan. 'Mrs Levy said two
for and one against', he pointed out to the Foreign Secretary,
'and that is correct', only to receive the answer, 'No, that is
not correct. I am not pro, nor am I anti.'

One's mind leaps back immediately to the Minister of
Propaganda in the Third Reich, Dr Josef Goebbels, a genius
who changed the art and tradition of public speaking. Addressing a meeting of farmers in Westphalia during the mid-
'thirties, he told them: 'We don't want higher bread prices.
We don't want lower bread prices. We don't want the same
bread prices. We want National Socialist bread prices.' The
applause which followed this splendid thought must have
been very gratifying to Dr Goebbels, who was not handi-
capped, of course, by having awkward people like Mrs Levy
and Mr Day on hand to inject a little common sense into the
occasion.

Public figures get away with their meaningless, evasive
statements much too easily, to the detriment of their mental
health. This is as true of the Prime Minister as of the Chairman of a Regional Gas or Electricity Board, the General
Secretary of the TUC – who is possibly the greatest living
master, at least in Britain, of saying nothing at all very impressively – the Director-General of the BBC, or the Chief

Executive of British Airways, all of whom are practised hands at rank-closing, standing evidence on its head and proving that white is black. This would not matter very much, perhaps, if they did not provide a model for thousands of lesser men, who can be excused for feeling that the way in which these obviously successful people go about things must, without a doubt, be right.

British Airways is no worse than any other national airline and its spokesmen are probably no more or less inclined than those of TWA, JAL or Qantas to indulge in diplomatic, executive-in-public language. But anyone who makes use of its services at all frequently would like to have straight-forward answers to these questions:

1. Why does one have to be so physically strong to use Heath-row airport? Why are the walking distances so great?

2. Why are British Airways' stewards and stewardesses, like those on the Americans' international routes, so impossibly, embarrassingly poor at foreign languages? Why is nothing done, so far as one can gather from the results, to recruit people who can speak at least passable French, German, Italian or Spanish and to teach them to improve? If no suitable natives are available, at any salary, why not employ foreigners with English to do the job?

3. Why, after all these years, are the seats so narrow and the leg-room so inadequate? Why should one be so much more uncomfortable in an aeroplane than in a train or a coach? Why does British Airways go on pretending to itself and to the travelling public that all its tourist class passengers are children or child-sized? Why do all other airlines do exactly the same? How have they managed to get away with such sadistic treatment for so long?

4. Why, if IATA regulations permit 'a piece of fruit' to be served with meals, is a piece of fruit never served?

5. Why is it never admitted by any airline that First Class is heavily subsidised by Tourist Class and never, in any year,

pays for itself? Why should First Class be subsidised at all by Tourist Class?

6. Why, despite all the safety evidence to support such a move, are rear-facing seats still not standard? Why does RAF Transport Command, the safest airline in the world, insist on rear-facing seats and why, if British Airways is so proud of Taking Good Care of You, does it not follow the RAF example?

7. Why, if it intends to persist in having forward-facing seats, does British Airways not pad the hard seat-backs, which are highly dangerous in the event of an accident?

8. Why does it go on insisting that the fastening of seat-belts is for passengers' safety, when all it is really for is to stop them walking about, getting in the way and changing the balance of the aircraft? Why does it choose to hide the fact that the most likely result of a tightly fastened seat belt, if an accident should occur, is a burst diaphragm or ruptured spleen, kidneys or liver? Why is the illusion of safety more important than safety itself?

And so on. The main reason why airline executives are so rarely asked fundamental questions like this by the media is that the media's flying public is made up very largely of people who travel in an aeroplane once a year to their holiday in Spain or the Western Mediterranean, the package-tour public. They are much more likely to use Gatwick or Luton than Heathrow, they go in aeroplanes which very rarely have any First Class accommodation, their journeys and their main worries, apart from flying at all, are concerned with surcharges, the exchange value of the pound, strikes and weary hold-ups at airports. Rear-facing seats and pieces of fruit never enter their consciousness and, since the television and newspaper editors know their market, the airline people get very little practice in talking in public about the things which annoy and puzzle regular travellers. When such inconvenient moments do occur, the usual tactics are to pretend that everyone, or at least everyone who matters, travels First

Class, where many of these inconveniences and irritations are less in evidence. The airline's method of keeping out of trouble is to give First Class anwers to Tourist Class questions, which can be annoying to the people who ask the questions. In any case, what is lost by dealing with questions in an honest way? Why should passengers continue to be duped about seat-belts, forward-facing seats and the rest? The image of the airline suffers, rather than gains from these we-are-perfect-stop-asking-stupid-questions approach.

The weakness of the conceal-as-much-as-possible-from-the-moronic-public approach is that the truth always does come out in the end and when it does it can boomerang and hit someone very hard indeed in the back of the neck. More important, it conditions the people responsible, making them feel instinctively that no mistakes or faults can ever be publicly admitted. If they mixed with a wider range of people or if their public relations department did its job properly, they would realise that most of the things they are so anxious to conceal have been generally known about for a long time already. Worse still, they might find that the public is, on some subjects, more intelligent than they suspected.

Most public relations men had the Vicar of Bray for a father. They are employed, as they see it, to put the best possible face on what the company is doing at the moment. They tell the public what they think it should know and keep the rest decently out of the way. While he is still managing director, Mr Jones is a summary of all the virtues and talents, but as soon as he is replaced by Mr Smith he turns out to have been something far less than perfect, certainly very inferior to Mr Smith. At one moment, something is impossible and crazy, and the world has to be told so as loudly and frequently as possible and at the next it is not only possible, but highly desirable and the company has been secretly planning to do it for years. Under such conditions, the unfortunate company spokesman needs to be able to pivot very rapidly on his axis.

There was a nice case of this in Cornwall, where, for many

years the china clay industry had been fouling up the rivers
and beaches with its milky processing-waste. There was no
denying that this was happening. One did not have to be any
kind of a specialist to see it. Company pronouncements therefore passed through a number of stages of development over
the years:

1. The situation has been grossly exaggerated. Waste does
   run away to sea, certainly, but it looks much worse than it
   is and there is no need to worry about it.

2. Yes, we admit this is rather unpleasant and we wish we
   could discover some way of preventing it from happening.
   But any preventive measures would be extremely expensive and might force us to increase our prices so much
   that sales would fall and people would be thrown out of
   jobs. And so, since we are the biggest employer in Cornwall
   and make such a large contribution to the local economy,
   Cornwall will have to put up with it and learn to live with
   the problem.

3. Technical advances and unceasing research have at last
   made it possible for us to be what we've always been most
   anxious to be, the Good Neighbour. Within a very short
   time, the streams will have their fish back and the beaches
   will be fit to walk on, thanks to our brilliant scientists,
   who are second to none in the country, and who have had
   the most generous and enthusiastic support from the Board.

Pragmatism is a sensible way of proceeding for much of the
time, but not all the time. 'Does it work?' and 'Can I get away
with it?' are dangerous questions, not so much because they
are an inadequate guide to doing the right thing, but because
one can never really know the answer. How does one know,
in the course of a television appearance, if one is getting away
with it or if it works? The interviewer may seem happy enough,
but that proves nothing. 'How many of the people watching
me and listening to me have seen through me?', our businessman should ask himself. 'Am I getting away with it?' This
can and should produce a state of mind very close to panic.

If, on the other hand, one is not trying to get away with anything, one can proceed with a serene mind, and one's performance will be greatly improved.

It should go without saying that the only audience one
should be concerned with is the primary audience, the
immediate audience. If it is a television occasion, it is the
television audience which matters, and that audience, one
should never forget, contains a very wide range of ages,
education, experience and intelligence and, most important
of all, it is 50 per cent female. The fact that the newspapers,
or some of them, will report your remarks or that your own
colleagues and friends may have tuned in may, if you remember it, help you to give a bad performance, but cannot
possibly help you to give a good one. For the time being,
forget about them and think hard of twenty people in a Tube
train or twenty people at a football match, or whatever your
own private symbol of a cross-section of people may happen
to be.

And, if your company should have the unpleasant and
unfair habit of confronting you with a transcript of what
you are supposed to have said at the meeting or while broadcasting, refuse to appear again on their behalf or choose
another employer. A transcript of something that was spoken
is a misleading and often useless record. It gives no idea of
which words and phrases were emphasised and which thrown
away, which parts were said smiling and which sternly and
gravely. If, in consequence, one is asked, 'Did you say
that, Robinson?', the only possible answer is 'Yes and no'.
'Those are the words I used, but there's no indication
whatever of how I said them or of the expression on my face
at that particular moment.' A sound-tape means much more
than a transcript and a video-tape much more still. A video-
tape, in fact, is a very good idea, not because it provides
evidence for the prosecution in the managing director's
court of law, but it allows one to make a valuable personal
check on one's performance.

There is, however, no telling how stupid one's employers

can be if they try. A few years ago, one of our six leading British companies issued a memorandum to its staff saying that, should any of them ever appear on television, in the company's name, they were not to smile. Business was a serious matter, and smiling could give altogether the wrong idea of how the company regarded its national function and its place in the community.

The best public performances are given by independent-spirited men and women, people who are not worried about getting another job if they should happen to lose this one. A private income is a great help, but few people have private incomes nowadays, and the next best thing is to make a point of always keeping in one's wallet or handbag, as a talisman, the advertisements of three jobs one would have a good chance of getting, should one choose to apply. The talisman should, of course, be kept up-to-date, or it loses its magic. And that magic consists of giving one the power to say, 'I don't care a damn what anybody else thinks, I'm going to do it my way'. Given that philosophy, one can be happy to appear in public. Without it, things are likely to go wrong from the beginning.

NOTES

1. City Literary Institute, London.
2. British Institute of Management.

Index

DATE DUE

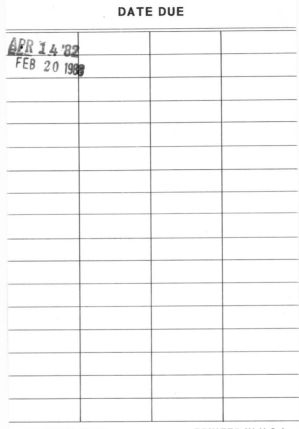

APR 14 '82

FEB 20 1988

HIGHSMITH 45-102   PRINTED IN U.S.A.